More Praise for

LIVING ZEN, LOVING GOD

"Free from dogmatism, Habito offers a vision for tackling the religious, ecological, and social issues of a world in deep crisis. This work provides inspiration for anyone seeking a spiritual path in global perspective."
—Professor Mark Unno, advisor to the
Journal of Buddhist-Christian Studies
and author of *Shingon Refractions*

"This book is a pioneering example of interspirituality: the experiential exploration of another tradition while remaining committed to one's own. Finding the common ground between the two traditions, Habito plunges into the depth of Zen and sheds new light on Christian faith. This is a very valuable book."
—Brother Wayne Teasdale, author of
The Mystic Heart and *A Monk in The World*

LIVING
ZEN,
LOVING
GOD

LIVING ZEN, LOVING GOD

RUBEN L.F. HABITO

FOREWORD BY JOHN P. KEENAN

Wisdom Publications • Boston

Wisdom Publications
199 Elm Street
Somerville MA 02144 USA
www.wisdompubs.org

Library of Congress Cataloging-in-Publication Data

Habito, Ruben L. F., 1947-
    Living Zen, loving God / Ruben L.F. Habito ; foreword by John P. Keenan.
        p. cm.
Includes bibliographical references and index
    ISBN 0-86171-383-4 (pbk. : alk. paper)
    1. Spiritual life—Zen Buddhism. 2. Spiritual life—Christianity. 3. Christianity and
other religions—Zen Buddhism. 4. Zen Buddhism—Relations—Christianity. I. Title
BQ9288 .H34 2004
261.2'43927—dc22

                                                            2003021351

Chapter nine is a revision of an essay previously published under the title "Zen and
Human Existence," in a volume edited by Hermann Haering and Johann Baptist Metz,
entitled *The Many Faces of the Divine* (SCM Press, 1995).

Other portions of this appeared in a different form as *Total Liberation.*

Cover design by Bob Aulicino
Interior design by Jane Grossett, Mindpage Design. Set in Garamond MT 11/13.

Wisdom Publications' books are printed on acid-free paper and meet the guidelines for permanence and durability of the Committee on Production Guidelines
for Book Longevity of the Council on Library Resources.

Printed in the United States of America.

To my father, Dr. Celestino P. Habito,

and mother, Faustina F. Habito (1921–1993),

with boundless gratitude for this gift of life.

Contents

Foreword

RUBEN HABITO IS A FINE SCHOLAR, well-trained and perceptive. More than that, though, he is an authentic practitioner of both Christianity and Zen. Even beyond *that,* Ruben has achieved a higher status — as quite an ordinary human being who loves his wife, plays with his young sons, and enjoys the good company of friends.

In a certain way, this book about living Zen and loving God maps the depths of Ruben Habito's ordinariness. As the Zen koan declares, "The ordinary mind is the path of awakening." Yet the claims of this book are bold. This is not a book *about* Buddhism and Christianity, or *about* emptiness and theism. Habito witnesses here to his experience of enlightenment through Zen practice. He also witnesses to his Christian faith. In another account, he has described his deep experience while a young man of expanding his awareness of God beyond the godfather figure that is so often mistaken for ultimate reality.[1] In this volume, he tells, simply and forthrightly, of the experience of awakening through the practice of Zen.

Remarkably, two recognized masters of the Japanese Sanbo Kyodan Zen lineage—Koun Yamada Roshi and Hakuun Yasutani Roshi—have validated this Christian Zen practitioner's enlightenment as authentic. As the famed German Jesuit and Zen master Father Hugo Enomiya-Lassalle observes in the foreword to the first and quite different edition of this book, Ruben Habito is the first Catholic whose experience of enlightenment was authenticated by recognized Zen masters. All of which certainly blurs the lines between being Christian and living Zen. A Jesuit practitioner immerses himself in Zen meditation practice and experiences not only deep and moving insight but instantiates the central, Buddha-making experience of enlightenment. This is a bold endeavor and an extraordinary claim, the more so when it is validated by the Zen masters assigned by the lineage to validate such experiences.

Usually things like this do not happen: Muslims rarely have visions of Vishnu. Jews do not encounter Jesus in the depths of their prayers. And even when people do claim to have cross-traditional religious experiences, they often remain suspect to the practitioners of those traditions. When the Yogi Yogananda Paramahamsa in his *Autobiography of a Yogi* recounts parallel visions of his teacher Iri Kukteswar and Jesus Christ, Christians tend to be highly skeptical—because Yogananda, in the context of his yogic metaphysics, describes the figures in his vision as astral bodies.[2] No Christian is likely to recognize him as a Christian on the basis of this vision.

But the Sanbo Kyodan headquarters, San-un Zendo (the Zen Hall of the Three Clouds) in Kamakura, where Habito began his Zen practice, is in some ways unique. It has a radical understanding of the Zen teaching that enlightenment is beyond words and is thus transmitted from person to person wordlessly—taking this to mean that such an experience of awakening is not restricted to persons who have a Buddhist affiliation. Jews and Christians, indeed anyone, can practice and can experience the depths first experienced by the Buddha Shakyamuni. This is indeed radical openness—rather like Christians offering to share their sacred Eucharistic communion with Buddhists, or recognizing the equal depths of grace and sanctity among Jews, Muslims, or Hindus. Not all would agree with such a bending of boundaries.

As Ruben Habito describes his experience of enlightenment, it was nested within its native Zen context in Japan and tested by Koun Yamada Roshi in the traditional private interview. It was further tested by Hakuun Yasutani Roshi, Yamada Roshi's teacher, and again declared to be authentic Zen enlightenment. Other non-Buddhists have since followed the same path, and there is now a small phalanx of Jewish and Christian Zen teachers trained in the Sanbo Kyodan lineage who have had similar experiences.

This is entirely different from the Zen that was exported to the West in the 1960s. A colleague once mentioned in conversation that he had asked revered Zen scholar D. T. Suzuki how many westerners had attained *satori*, enlightenment, during his many years of teaching in America. "Not one!" Suzuki replied. He felt that Zen was part and parcel of Japanese culture, outside of which it was difficult to practice and almost impossible to practice effectively. That would be the typical attitude of most traditions—that people first have to be culturally prepared to hear and practice the true path. Indeed, Christians often identify their (Western) culture with the gospel itself.

But in this volume we do not read about boundary theory at all. We do not talk about Buddhism and Christianity. Rather we read about living and loving, as interwoven in a Catholic Christian culture and Church and a Zen Buddhist lineage and meditation hall. We read about life-transforming experiences, about enlightenment that goes beyond boundaries and religious affiliation.[3]

Yet there is no mixing of traditions here. Each remains clear and distinct, even though interwoven in the practices of loving God and living Zen. Each tradition enriches the other without either turning into some sort of bastardized mutation of itself. Ruben Habito likes to describe his understanding of these two traditions as the mutual indwelling of living Zen and loving God. The term he employs comes from a Greek theological word, *perichoresis*, which is used in Christian theology to describe the complete and total indwelling of each of the persons of the Trinity in the other persons, so that Father, Son, and Spirit—while distinct from one another—fully dwell within the one encompassing reality described as the Trinity. So here, Zen remains Zen and Christian faith remains Christian faith. Neither is watered down. Neither is confused or bent out of shape. Rather each interweaves with and dwells within the other.

The Zen practice of Ruben Habito is not the ethereal Zen of the popular imagination that lies somehow beyond any concrete religious practice or teaching. It is the Zen taught in the Sanbo Kyodan by the Japanese masters Yasutani and Yamada, as learned and practiced by a number of North American teachers—Sister Elaine MacInnes, Bernie Glassman, Father Robert Kennedy, and others. Likewise, the Catholic faith expressed here is not a diminished faith somehow made to fit into the Zen patterns of teaching. That is not what *Living Zen, Loving God* is about. Quite the contrary, each tradition here is driven toward its most gut-wrenching experience, and all practice is aimed at witnessing the inner reality of the tradition. The Chinese Zen master Wu-men in his *Gateless Gate* comments on the koan "Three Pounds of Flax" by saying that Old Man Tung-shan has really exposed his innards, just as an opened clam exposes his liver and intestines. Wu-men is not offering a doctrinal teaching here about Buddha-nature but pointing directly to the gut-wrenching experience of living enlightenment, of living Zen, of loving God.

And such gut-wrenching experience, in its turn, coaxes forth insights into doctrinal truths. When Ruben Habito speaks of loving God and explains that God is at the same time subject, object, and the very act of loving, he references not only Augustine, but even more Wu-men, for such an experience describes a trinity of non-discriminative circumincession, wherein the one all-encompassing, and yet empty, love of God drives us toward enlightenments that reengage us in this concrete world.

This perichoretic theology holds traditions in creative tension within the personal practice of an individual history. Its emptiness is grounded in the dependently arisen history of each and every practitioner. Ruben Habito was born in Asia, raised in the Catholic tradition of the Philippines, formed by the exercises of St. Ignatius Loyola, immersed in Japanese culture and philosophy, and trained in a Zen meditation hall to struggle with the koan "Mu" (A monk asked Chao-chou "Has the dog Buddha-nature or not?' Chao-chou said, "Mu." [Nah!]). That koan triggered an experience so authentic in Habito that it elicited the stamp of authenticity from Zen masters adept at discerning authentic insight from false states of awakening. This uniquely personal history of Ruben Habito gives rise to the tensions in this book—not unhealthy tensions but creative ones, the kind of tensions that might well arise within a Christian practitioner drawn to practice zazen and take his own Buddha-nature as an existential reality.

The theology I see in *Living Zen, Loving God* can rightly be termed "inchoate theology," a theology of insights wrenched out of intense practice, engaged in the world, hesitant to reach final verbal statement, always driving one back toward the deepest core of what it means to be human. It refuses to rush toward conceptual clarity, for the great and constant danger of religions is to grasp in words what one has hardly even begun to experience in one's innards. And although Zen does indeed have a verbal history and a developed tradition, as many scholars have pointed out,[4] that tradition impels one toward total liberation, both personal and social, both ultimate and worldly.

This is a groaning theology, one that struggles through hours of practice and sitting to express what clear words often hide. The Zen tradition is rich in stories of disciples and masters who answer one another with shouts, blows, and grunts, with deep visceral images that do express things but refuse to circumscribe the Buddha mind within any easy grasp. Just so, Saint Paul writes that this world is groaning and struggling until it reaches its fullness, in Christ.

John P. Keenan
Steep Falls, Maine
Winter 2004

JOHN P. KEENAN is a Canon of the Anglican church and is one of the editors of *Beside Still Waters: Jews, Christians, and the Way of the Buddha* as well as *The Gospel of Mark: A Mahayana Reading.*

1 "Close Encounters of a Certain Kind," in *Beside Still Waters: Jews, Christians, and the Way of the Buddha*. Edited by Harold Kasimow, John P. Keenan, & Linda Klepinger Keenan (Boston: Wisdom Publications, 2003).

2 Yogananda, Paramahamsa, *The Autobiography of a Yogi* (Self-Realization Fellowship, 1944), p. 475 ff. and 561 ff.

3 The reader is encouraged to delve into James W. Heisig's provocative *Dialogues at One Inch Above the Ground: Reclamations of Belief in an Interreligious Age* (Crossroads, 2003).

4 Among others see Bernard Faure, *The Rhetoric of Immediacy: A Cultural Critique of Chan/Zen Buddhism* (Princeton University Press, 1991); Steven Heine, ed., with Dale W. Wright, *The Koan: Text and Context in Zen Buddhism* (Oxford University Press, 2000) and Steven Heine, *Opening a Mountain: Koans of the Zen Masters* (Oxford University Press, 2002); John McRae, *The Northern School and the Formation of Early Ch'an Buddhism* (University of Hawaii Press, 1986) and Robert H. Sharf, *Coming to Terms with Chinese Buddhism: A Reading of the Treasure Store Treatise* (University of Hawaii, 2001).

Foreword to the First Edition

IT IS WITH GREAT JOY THAT I offer a foreword to the compilation of Zen material by Ruben Habito. When Ruben Habito arrived in Japan in 1970, he almost immediately became involved in Zen. He was, as far as I know, the first Catholic to have received confirmation of the opening Zen experience (*kensho*) under a Japanese Zen master. Since then he assiduously maintained his training under this true teacher, Koun Yamada Roshi of the Kamakura San-un Zendo.

During his formative years as a Jesuit in Japan, Ruben proved himself of high intellectual caliber by being admitted to the prestigious University of Tokyo, and acquitting himself honorably amid its erudition, completing doctoral studies in Buddhist philosophy.

Ruben Habito is eminently equipped to write this book. I refer not only to his knowledge of Buddhism and Christianity and his practical experience of sitting in Zen meditation, but more particularly to the deepening in his Zen practice resulting in the deepening of his social concern.

Reading this work, I am impressed by the way the he shows that our experiences in Zen are confirmed in the life and words of Jesus Christ as they are laid down in the Gospels. I am convinced that readers of this book will enjoy it and be helped to understand better the relation between Zen and Christian spirituality.

Hugo M. Enomiya-Lassalle, S.J.

Preface

THE ESSAYS IN THIS COLLECTION are my attempts to address the following questions: What is the nature of the Zen enlightenment experience? How does this experience help guide our actions in the world, laden as it is with conflict and violence and suffering? How does the experience of enlightenment ground a socially engaged spirituality? And coming to Zen practice as one born and raised in a Christian (specifically Roman Catholic) tradition, I address a question that comes out of my own inner struggle over many years: How am I to understand and articulate the Zen experience in the light of my own Christian faith?

A tentative answer to this last question is suggested in the title of this new edition of this book: *Living Zen, Loving God.* To venture a *very* short version here, living the life of Zen in an authentic way is to experience what Christians refer to in using the phrase "loving God." However, it must be made clear again and again that the term *God* used in this context is not to be taken merely as an object of the verb *loving*. In fact it is the subject, the object, as well as the very act of Loving itself. But again the Buddhist in me immediately jumps in with a rejoinder: In making such a claim, one needs to realize, and emphasize, that the subject, the object, and the act, are all empty!

The above "answer" is obviously unsatisfactory in its awkward formulation, so I invite the reader to walk with me through these essays for a glimpse of what I would like to convey.

May these essays, culled from my own Zen talks and writings over the years, and now revised extensively for Wisdom Publications, help the reader toward a better understanding of the possibilities as well as the perils and pitfalls of Zen practice and its implications for daily life in our troubled world. May they call attention to an aspect that has largely been left undeveloped in many treatments of Zen, namely its empowering significance for socially engaged praxis. And finally, may they enable the reader to see resonances with themes in Christian spirituality, so that those who come from or find their home in the Christian tradition may be able to rediscover and celebrate the underlying treasures therein.

Acknowledgments

I WOULD LIKE to express my deepest gratitude to my late teacher, Koun Yamada Roshi, whose continuing presence and guidance can be felt throughout the pages of this book, and to his wife, Mrs. Kazue Yamada, a generous and warmhearted mother to us all who sat in zazen at San-un Zendo.

Profound gratitude also to Jiun Kubota Roshi and Ryoun Yamada Roshi, his successors in leading Sanbo Kyodan, who continue to keep the lamp of the Dharma alive in our lineage. Special thanks go to all my Dharma sisters and brothers in the Sanbo Kyodan community of teachers, from whom I receive so much guidance and wisdom and many warm hugs, as we meet one another in our annual retreats and workshops. Among these, I would like to thank Sister Elaine MacInnes, OLM, in a special way. It was at her invitation that I had the opportunity to offer Zen talks to her sangha in Manila, out of which many of the essays in this collection grew. A deep bow and gassho in thanks for her continuing friendship and guidance through the years.

My deep gratitude goes to so many individuals, but in particular:

To the late Father Hugo Enomiya-Lassalle, S.J., who graciously wrote the foreword to the first edition, and was a pioneer who opened the way for many in the path of Zen. To Father Thomas Hand, S.J., who, as my spiritual director in my early years of Jesuit formation, introduced me to Yamada Roshi and the Sanbo Kyodan community in Kamakura.

To Robert Aitken Roshi, mentor and elder Dharma brother, who offered wholehearted support in my move from Japan to the United States, and who encouraged me to "water the dry plains of the Southwest." For me as for so many others he is an embodiment of the Zen life of wisdom that flows out into compassion.

To Sister Rosario Battung, RGS, a Dharma sister, who literally took me by the hand and introduced me to many of the people she worked with in Isabela, the northern part of the Philippines, wherein took place many memorable and heartwarming encounters that continue to inform who I am now.

To Sister Vicky Palanca, friend and support through the years.

To Joan Rieck, a Dharma sister who also lives in the plains of the Southwest, who graciously agrees to come and sit with us from time to time and offer her gentle guiding hand to members of our Maria Kannon Zen community in Dallas, Texas.

To all the members of our Maria Kannon Zen community who have sat with us through the years, for being an intimate part of my Zen journey. They have been my teachers in this path of Zen. A special note of gratitude and appreciation goes to Helen Cortes, for her selfless and devoted service to the sangha, and without whom we would not be where we are today.

To each and everyone in my immediate family, beginning with my parents, to whom I dedicate this book, my brothers and sisters and their families, to my spouse, Maria Dorothea, and sons Florian and Benjamin.

To Robert Ellsberg and William Burrows, of Orbis Books, who kindly allowed the publication of the much earlier edition of this book in 1989.

To my Zen teacher colleagues David Loy, Taigen Leighton, Mitra Bishop, James Ishmael Ford, and others, who nudged me to take steps toward the re-publication of this book that had been several years out of print, and sent in kind words on my behalf to Wisdom Publications. And last but not least, to Josh Bartok, my editor at Wisdom, my heartfelt thanks for his encouraging words, wise advice, and pointed questions and comments. His unsparing efforts have made a tremendous difference in enhancing the quality and precision in expression of the essays in this collection.

Introduction

THE JAPANESE TERM *kensho* is often translated as "enlightenment experience"—though in Japanese, it is written as a compound of two characters meaning "to see" and "one's own nature." Thus, enlightenment in the Zen context is understood as an experience of "seeing into one's own nature," that is, seeing through, and seeing clearly, the reality of everything as not separate from oneself, of everything as it really is.

Kensho is the pivotal second "fruit" of the "three fruits" of zazen, or the practice of seated meditation. The first fruit, the deepening of the power of concentration *(joriki)*, paves the way for enlightenment, and the third, personalization of this enlightenment—described as the "bodily manifestation of the peerless way" *(mujodo no taigen)*—flows out of it.

The essays in this collection are attempts at unpacking these experiences and examining them from different angles.

The first essay, entitled "Seeing into One's Nature," is an account of my own initial glimpse of the world of Zen, describing an experience of kensho that was confirmed by my teacher, Yamada Roshi. This essay also reflects my early attempts at articulating the Zen enlightenment experience in terms of the Christian faith tradition that I was raised in and continue to belong to.

The second essay, "Emptiness and Fullness," focuses on how one's experience of enlightenment affects and throws light on our entire worldview and our relationship to world events. The Buddhist scriptural image of the mirror as a way of describing the awakened mind, presented in this chapter, offers a clue as to how Zen enlightenment can ground a socially engaged spirituality, which in turn can empower a person to plunge effectively into the world of suffering beings and seek ways to attain liberation with them.

The third essay, "The Heart Sutra on Liberating Wisdom," offers a reading of the Heart Sutra, a short scriptural text regularly chanted in Zen halls throughout the world, as a way of articulating the Zen enlightenment experience. The Heart Sutra is highly regarded throughout Mahayana Buddhist history as a succinct expression of the nature, structure, and "content" of the Buddha's enlightenment—and of reality itself. Its central message is cached in the phrase "Form is no other than emptiness, emptiness no other than form." This essay examines the experiential dimension of this phrase. The first part looks at the cause of our suffering, our clinging to finite realities of "form," and the source of our liberation from suffering, namely realizing the emptiness of all form. The second part of this essay describes a return to these finite realities in a way devoid of attachment. This is the return of the bodhisattva, with a heart of compassion that embraces all beings, to this world of suffering.

The fourth essay, taking a straight look at the mystery of suffering, explores a famous koan from Master Yunmen that appears in the *Blue Cliff Record*: "Every day is a good day." Usually the treatment of a koan is reserved to the one-to-one encounters between a Zen student and a qualified Zen teacher, but this open treatment of a particular koan may serve to elucidate what "working with a koan" involves, without revealing material reserved for oral transmission.

The fifth essay elucidates Hakuin's "Song of Zazen," a work popular especially in Rinzai Zen circles. We will recall Christian themes as we explore Hakuin's meaning. The poem's opening line and central theme, that "all sentient beings are originally Buddhas," articulates the content of the Great Faith (or Great Trust) that, together with Great Doubt and Great Resolve, form a threesome to serve as the keys to the realization of enlightenment.

The sixth essay, "The Enlightened Samaritan," is a Zen reading of a narrative from New Testament scriptures, the well-known Parable of the Good Samaritan, seeking to overcome the moralistic stereotypes associated with this story, and hoping to bring forth its message of an enlightened way of being and how this relates to living a life of compassion in this world

The seventh essay explores the Four Vows of the Bodhisattva. It lays out the implications of these vows for a way of life that is characterized by a heart and mind that embraces all sentient beings, and actively works for their liberation. This is another classic expression of an awakened mind and compassionate heart that grounds a socially engaged spirituality and worldview.

The eighth essay looks closely at the Bodhisattva Kanzeon, "Regarder of the Cries of the World," also known as Kannon (Kuan Yin or Guanyin in Chinese, Avalokiteshvara in Sanskrit). In Kanzeon we find a powerful inspiration for Buddhist social and ecological engagement, which in many ways parallels the figure of Mary in the Christian tradition.

The ninth essay, "Zen Experience of Triune Mystery," examines the three crucial "moments" in the Zen way of life and notes resonances with a Christian theme of life lived in the inner circle of the Triune Mystery.

The final essay is a brief account of how Zen practice, centered on attunement with the breath, resonates with the central themes of an engaged Christian spirituality. Particular attention is given to the relation between Zen practice and the fulfillment of the mission of Jesus to bring light to those who cannot see, and to liberate the poor and oppressed of this earth. (Luke 4:16–31)

An appendix is offered, which is a transcription of a conversation between Koun Yamada Roshi and Father Hugo Enomiya Lassalle, S.J., two spiritual giants, now deceased, who continue to be a source of inspiration for the author. The issues addressed in this conversation with these two Zen masters, one a Buddhist, the other a Christian, relate intimately to the central themes of this volume.

Seeing into
One's Nature:
A CHRISTIAN'S EXPERIENCE OF ZEN

I WAS FIRST INTRODUCED TO ZEN in the spring of 1971, less than a year after arriving in Japan from the Philippines. A Japanese friend invited me to join a Zen retreat (called *sesshin*, literally, "encounter of the heart") to be held at Engakuji, a Rinzai temple in Kita-Kamakura. Curious and fascinated, I found myself plunged into a four-day period of rigorous discipline, rising at 3:00 A.M. and continuing until 10 P.M., meditating in strict silence broken only by the sounds of bells and wooden clappers and the shouted calls to attention from the senior monks. Time was spent mainly just sitting in lotus position in a large hall, paying attention to my breath.

I came out of it with aching legs and a back sore from the trainer-monks' "encouragement stick" (called *keisaku* or *kyosaku,* literally "warning device." Yet my first retreat was a powerful and exhilarating experience that whetted my appetite for more.

It was auspicious that my then-current Jesuit spiritual director, Father Thomas Hand, S.J., was also practicing Zen, and it was he who introduced me to Koun Yamada, the roshi (Zen master) in charge of the lay community of practitioners who came to sit at the San-un Zendo in Kamakura.

At my initial interview or *dokusan,* as the roshi asked me what I sought in taking up this practice of Zen, I replied that I wanted to know the answer to the question "Who am I?" With this he gave me the famous *mu*-koan for my Zen practice. The *mu*-koan goes thus:

A monk asked Zen Master Chao-chou in all earnestness: "Has a dog Buddha-nature or not?" Chao-chou answered, "Mu!"

I was then instructed to set aside all thoughts about the dog, or of Buddha-nature, and just take Chao-chou's response as my cue, repeating it with each outbreath as I sat in zazen facing a wall. Hold onto this *mu,* Roshi told me. Come back to it repeatedly and let it accompany me as I lay down to sleep.

It was only a couple of weeks after this, amid my intensified daily practice of zazen, that I was struck by an experience like an earth-shaking flash of lightning. I burst into laughter and simultaneously shed tears of joy. The impact of that experience lasted for several days afterward. Yamada Roshi, probing me with the usual checking questions for kensho experience, later confirmed during dokusan that this was a genuine *kensho* or Zen enlightenment experience. Hakuun Yasutani Roshi, his predecessor and teacher, who was visiting Kamakura at that time, likewise made a similar confirmation in another interview, being satisfied with my answers to his questions about the character of the experience I recounted. This event, these teachers told me, marked my formal entry into the world of Zen. Nurtured by further sitting and years of additional koan practice, this initial experience continued to deepen, and to illuminate my whole existence in all its particulars.

But how am I to describe this experience? Trying to describe kensho is as futile as trying to meaningfully convey the experience of tasting green tea. Most usefully I can only point to a hot cup of tea and invite others to drink and taste it themselves.

Similarly, the real message of the Gospels is not a mere description of a state of affairs, but rather an invitation to taste and see how good is the Lord!, to "come and behold the wondrous deeds of God" (Psalms 46:8). The Gospels' words and concepts at best serve an invitational function to a living encounter with divine Presence right at the heart of our humanity.

In the introductory talks for prospective Zen practitioners, one is told of the three fruits of Zen. These are: the development of the power of concentration, or samadhi *(joriki);* the attainment of enlightenment, or awakening *(kensho-godo);* and the manifestation of enlightenment in everyday life *(mujodo no taigen).* The discipline of sitting and simply paying attention to one's breath naturally brings forth the first fruit, as one is able to "center" one's whole existence in the here and now of every breath, bringing together all the mental, emotional, psychological, and other elements that constitute our personality and otherwise tend to get dispersed in our usual hectic daily lives. A strengthened power of concentration is a natural result of disciplined attention and awareness, in sitting as well as in the activities of daily life. One who practices zazen for a considerable period of time tends toward a greater integration in one's life, bringing the pieces together, so to speak, toward a wholeness that is also wholesomeness.

This integration and development of concentration sets the conditions for what is truly pivotal in Zen: the experience of enlightenment. Enlightenment is not, of course, attained solely by virtue of the sheer amount of time one spends in sitting practice, though this sitting certainly helps. To put it in Christian terms, kensho can only be described as a marvelous work of grace. We cannot bring about this experience through our striving, rather we can only dispose ourselves toward the occurrence of this event of grace by means of assiduously practicing zazen, attending to our breathing, and attuning ourselves to the here and now.

Yet all the years of sitting and disciplined practice do not guarantee the "results" as such. Similar experiences can and do happen to individuals who have never formally sat in Zen. God in total freedom can make children of Abraham from stones, as a New Testament saying goes (Matthew 3:9). All of us in the proper time are susceptible to that visit of grace; all we can do from our side is simply dispose ourselves by striving to remove as many obstacles as we humanly can.

The experience of enlightenment is sometimes described in this way: The chick still enveloped in the eggshell attempts to wiggle out from within, pecking away at the inside of the shell with its own little beak. Then, at the opportune time, the mother hen pecks the egg from the outside, and *lo!*—the shell is broken and the chick comes out into the light! The single timely "peck" from a Zen master is all that is required to free us from our inordinate desires and basic ego attachment.

Then we set about attempting to order our lives in the way of Zen discipline; once the shell is cracked, the chick must continue the process of becoming a full-grown chicken. The third fruit of Zen is thus described as the personalization of the enlightenment experience in our daily lives, as we enable it to shed light on every nook and cranny of our day-to-day world. The breakthrough to the initial experience is like getting hold of a key to open the first koan and finding that it is a master key that opens all the other doors as well! Further work with koans amounts to learning to use that key to open other doors set before us in an exciting process of discovery that lets us go deeper and deeper into the mystery of our very being, the mystery of the universe. And yet koan practice is a process that keeps us going back to where we have always been right from the start.

I must admit, though, to having had somewhat of a headstart when I began Zen practice. I had been introduced to the Ignatian spiritual exercises when I entered the Society of Jesus in the early sixties. During my novitiate days in the Philippines, I had the privilege of undergoing the thirty-day Ignatian Exercises. This was my formal introduction to Jesuit spirituality, and to a way of life that included an hour of daily meditative silence. An annual eight-day period of spiritual practice in the Ignatian tradition was part of the regimen that I had been accustomed to for many years previous to beginning Zen.

However, the Ignatian Exercises, especially during the initial stage, tend to place an emphasis on efforts of the discursive mind, calling for a great deal of theological conceptualization and reflection.

Coming to Zen practice—being told to do away with all such conceptualizing and mental effort and to just sit with my breathing — opened the windows of my being, letting wonderfully fresh air come in. This was for me the living Breath of God, which recreates the earth and makes all things new. Theological ideas are but pictures of, say, a delicious piece of sweet dumpling, which may perhaps make the mouth water but can never fill a hungry stomach. Zen practice invites us to set aside the picture, grab the dumpling, and take a bite.

At first, when working on the koan Mu that led to my experience of kensho, I was inclined to approach it through elaborate intellectual gymnastics, having been trained in philosophy in my Jesuit formation and also being of a rather inquisitive temperament. The original context of the koan is simply a negative response of Chao-chou to the monk's question: "No, dear monk, a dog does *not* have Buddha-nature."

But then, of course, this goes against basic Buddhist doctrine, which affirms the Buddha-nature (or original nature, or "essential" nature) in all living beings, including dogs and cats, salamanders and cockroaches, and everything else. Moreover, the word *mu* also means "nothing." And so the koan set me "thinking" about the concept of "nothing" or of "nothingness," and I could not help but philosophize about this notion both during and outside of my Zen sitting.

Incidentally, during that time that I had begun Zen practice with the *mu*-koan, I was reading a book in Japanese by the renowned Kyoto School philosopher Nishitani Keiji, later translated in English with the title *Religion and Nothingness*. From this reading, I received the very important hint that this *mu* is not the same as the *concept* of "nothingness" or "nonbeing" that is simply in opposition to "being." I began to see that Chao-chou's *mu* transcends this dualism: It is neither "something" nor "nothing" and is beyond "being" and "nonbeing."

Thus, in my zazen, I gave up my mental efforts at trying to analyze the concepts involved, and I simply sat—with my legs crossed, straightening my back, regulating my breathing, putting my whole being to focus on this *mu* with the outbreath. Roshi encouraged me in interviews "to become one with" *mu,* to become *totally absorbed (botsunyu:* literally, "to lose oneself and enter") into it. *Mu* and only *mu. Mu* with every breath. Likewise, *mu* with every step, every smile, every touch, every sensation.

And it was this frame of mind that precipitated that explosive experience that would enlighten my whole being—and indeed the whole universe!

☾

This experience changed my relationship to certain Christian teachings, such as the "doctrine" of *creatio ex nihilo,* creation from nothing.

In the light of kensho, *creatio ex nihilo* is for me no longer a mere philosophical or theological concept or doctrine that merely states that "Once upon a time there was nothing and thence came something" or some other such simplistic formulation. I came to see it as a very suggestive expression of an ever-present wonderment, with every breath, every step, every smile...every leaf, every flower, every raindrop, realized as literally as *nothing* but the grace-filled gift from the infinite and ever-flowing divine love!

In other words, everything in the whole universe—leaves, rocks, mountains, living beings of every sort—is simply and originally *nothing* other than the freely given gift from a divine source, uttered into being every moment by the Word, by Logos, "through whom all things came into being, and without whom not one thing came into being" (John 1:3). Everything, in its own particularity, is in a relationship of absolute dependence upon the Infinite source of all that is. Further, nothing at all exists apart from this Infinite source of all that is. In short, it is this Infinite source "in whom we live and move and have our being" (Acts 17:28).

As one realizes one's own nothingness in the face of this Infinite Mystery, one is thereby opened to an experience of one's nothingness, which is also an experience of the divine presence permeating through this nothingness, beyond the concept of "nothing" and the concept of "being."

We can see this sentiment echoed in the "fourfold negation" of the great second-century Mahayana Buddhist philosopher Nagarjuna:

"It" is not being, not nonbeing, not both being and nonbeing, nor neither being and nonbeing. To "see" it thus is to see into one's true nature, one's original nature, or in the terms of Chao-chou's mu, "Buddha-nature."

In Christian terms, our original nature can perhaps be called our *Christ nature*. A biblical passage from the Letter to the Ephesians articulates it in this way: God has chosen us in Christ, before the foundation of the world, to be holy and blameless before God, in love" (Ephesians 1:4). We can thus speak of our "Christ nature" as the most constitutive of who we are, having been so right from the foundation of the world, or even before. In the Zen terms of another koan, Christ nature is "our original face, before our father and mother were born."

Philosophical musings on the *notion* of Buddha-nature or the original face would miss the point, and so would musings on the theological implications of the "meaning" of *Christ nature,* or the doctrine of *creatio ex nihilo*. We are invited to set aside our recipe books or menus, and simply "taste and see" for ourselves.

I recall a Catholic sister who came to a profound experience that brought her to tears during a Zen retreat. The words that came welling up from the depths, accompanied by profuse tears of joy, were "I am innocent." She was indeed gifted with a glimpse of her "original nature," as she was able to experience this realm of the "holy and blameless" in her practice of silent sitting.

Zen enlightenment can also be described as an experience of "dying to one's old self" and being reborn into an entirely new life. For the Christian, this is an event that enables one to experience the Paschal Mystery of Christ's death and resurrection (Romans 6:3–4; Colossians 2:12; Philippians 3:10; 1 Peter 3:18–22) *in this very body*. To live in the newness of life in Christ (2 Corinthians 5:15, 17) is to partake of the divine life in oneself. From the depths of one's being, truly one exclaims with Paul that "it is no longer I that live, but Christ in me!" (Galatians 2:20).

Living in this dimension, one realizes what it is to live as the "body of Christ," given life by the same Breath, the same Spirit: "So we, though many, are one body in Christ, and individually members one of another" (Romans 12:5). This realization has tremendous implications in the social, cultural, political, economic spheres of our lives, for now there is no one and nothing that is not an essential part of my very self. Realizing this, we see, as the modern sage Krishnamurti put it, that we are the totality of what the world is; the world is the totality of what we are. Thus, just as the pain in my little finger is felt by my whole body, *I cannot but* be concerned with all that is going on in this world of ours, with all the pain, suffering, and cries of anguish of so many living beings. They are *my* pain and *my* suffering.

The realization of one's "Christ-nature" involves dying to the "old" self—dying to all our ego-centered attachments, and being reborn to a newness of life "in Christ." This rebirth concretely affects choices in our way of life, our values, our particular preferences in this existence at this time and place in history. In the words of Saint Ignatius of Loyola, it is "to be poor with Christ poor, to be despised with Christ despised."

A deeper and deeper appreciation of our "Christ nature" can be experienced with the contemplation of the life of Jesus, the one "in whom the fullness of God was pleased to dwell" (Colossians 1: 19). As we contemplate the life of Jesus, his experience is revealed to us bodily. This is a mode of spiritual exercise recommended by Ignatius in the second phase (the second week) of his Spiritual Exercises, after the first phase of purification. To contemplate on the life of Jesus of Nazareth is to take this life as a divine revelatory event, and as the archetype and model for one's own life, seeking to experience total unity with Christ with the totality of one's own being. This means taking the path Jesus took, and making the same fundamental choices he made. It also means living one's life as opened to the Breath, in proclaiming the Good News to the poor, in announcing release to the captives, in recovering sight for those who cannot see, in setting the captives free (Luke 4:18–19).

One who accepts this Christ nature as one's own is one who places one's life with Jesus on the side of the poor, the oppressed of the earth in the concrete realm of earthly existence, proclaiming the message of liberation and salvation, and accepting the consequences of this message as Jesus did.

So to experience being "one in Christ" with all beings involves not only a oneness in eating and drinking and laughing and crying with all sentient beings, but also a concrete experience of solidarity with the sufferings of living beings in this historical existence. This is the solidarity that Jesus the Christ himself assumed with the sufferings of all humankind on the Cross.

To contemplate the Cross of Christ, a long-standing mode of Christian prayer and spiritual practice, is not a sadistic or masochistic enterprise that relishes the sight of suffering. Rather, it enables one to open to a spiritual experience of plunging into the lot of suffering humankind, as Christ did on the Cross. It is also a call to behold and see as one's own the concrete ways in which living beings suffer or are made to suffer in our present day and age—to look at the poverty and hunger, at the destitution and deprivation, at the discrimination and oppression, at the various forms of structural, physical, and all kinds of violence that desecrate this sacred gift of human life.

To be one with this suffering and death of Christ on the Cross is also to be one in the newness of life as the Risen One. This solidarity with suffering men and women and children throughout the world is the source of the energy that enables us to give ourselves fully in the specific tasks of liberating beings in specific historical contexts. Thus, contemplation on the Risen One gives the vision that all this suffering is *not* in vain, that it does not all end in defeat and desperation, but in glorification and triumph. Right here, in the midst of apparent defeat and despair, is the vision of glory. It is on the Cross itself that Jesus tells the Good Thief beside him, "Truly, today you are with me in Paradise" (Luke 23:43).

To see into one's true nature is an experience of Mystery that goes beyond all breadth and length and height and depth (Ephesians 3:18–19) with boundless treasures (Colossians 2:2–3, Romans 11:33).

After passing through the gateless gate of the initial enlightenment experience, the Zen practitioner is guided into further koan practice by a Zen master trained in the use of koans. Further koan practice enables one to continue fathoming the depths and scaling the heights of the world of enlightenment, as one incarnates the Mystery in one's concrete, everyday life. There is no thought, word, or action that does not become its concrete expression. Sitting, walking, drinking tea, doing menial tasks, washing one's face, looking at the stars, talking to a friend—everything becomes inundated with a *fullness,* precisely as one is *emptied* of oneself in every thought, word, action.

In summary, Zen enlightenment does not usher one into a world of euphoric contentment and stoic detachment, as some might imagine. Zen is not a spiritual practice that shields one from the realities of this world to provide a haven of peace and security within one's own small self. Rather, Zen enlightenment involves a stance of readiness to plunge right into the very heart of the world, in solidarity with all the joys and hopes; the pains and sufferings; the blood, sweat, and tears of all sentient beings—right here and now.

Emptiness
and Fullness

"IN A WORD, TELL ME, WHAT IS ZEN TO YOU?" asked someone who had heard that I had been into Zen practice. Actually, the most apt answer I could have given would have been, "Good evening," or "How's your wife today?" or "Let's have some coffee." Or even, "Well…"

And contrary to appearances, this would not have been an evasion of my friend's sincere question. Each of these responses, in their concreteness and irreducibility, is in itself fully the manifestation of the inexhaustible reality that Zen opens to all. And yet, there is also no word that can even *approach* this reality. Words in their conventional sense are only *signs* that can never fully capture what they aim to convey—a fact we must keep in mind in pursuing even the series of words in this book!

But, given this caution, let me venture another answer to the question. A very provisional answer is that, for me, Zen, in a word, is simply *"Emptying."*

Let me now try to unpack this word. I ask the reader's forbearance in engaging in what is regarded in Zen as "talking dirty"—using conceptual language in the attempt to describe what basically can never be reduced to a concept. More often than not, this kind of language only manages to hide rather than reveal.

In our everyday lives we find our conscious selves "filled" with many things—memories of yesterday or yesteryear both bitter and sweet; plans for tomorrow or for our next vacation; thoughts about grandiose projects and menial tasks; worries about our relationships with family, the demanding professor at school, the unappreciative boss at the office; concerns about how we are going to make ends meet. Furthermore, the media fills our thoughts with imagery both rich and trivial: the crime rate, the economic situation, this coming sports event, the movie or book that is the talk of the town, and so forth. All these elements demand our attention and pull us in many different directions.

As our conscious minds are filled with these things, these unavoidable elements in our everyday world, we at times get certain twinges of a forlorn feeling that living our lives "merely" on this level is incomplete, superficial, unsatisfying. Such feelings offer us a faint suggestion that there must be something more to life than all this. And such twinges lead us to question the quality of our lives as lived on this level of consciousness. They enable us to pose the question of whether there may not be a *deeper* dimension within ourselves that heretofore we have not been aware of, much less concerned with.

Asking such questions may lead us to seek answers in reading psychology and self-help books. And these answers can of course offer helpful insights about our lives in our relationships with others and in our emotional ups and downs, in our deep-seated anxieties and insecurities, and in our need for affective support and adequate affective expression. Some such books may also tell us of another level of consciousness to be explored, the "unconscious" wherein reside our dreams, our most deeply cherished hopes, our unexpressed reserves and conflicts. They may tell us how to overcome such conflicts, how to resolve unconscious tensions within us, how to accept ourselves and accept others, and so on.

And thus both the conscious *and* unconscious levels of what we call our "self" become filled with so many things that divide our existence into disparate elements—and still we find that we are craving a wholeness that would unite these elements, a wholeness that would enable us to experience life as meaningful, worthwhile, joyful, beautiful.

Where are we to go in seeking this wholeness and inner peace for which our whole being yearns, "as a deer yearns for running streams" (Psalm 42)?

The Buddhist tradition, in agreement with many other of the world's wisdom traditions, tells us that what we are looking for is not to be found by looking outside ourselves. Our yearning is not fulfilled in the satisfaction of a material want, in this or that pleasurable sensation, in this or that philosophical idea, however sublime, in this or that religious or theological concept.

What we are really seeking deep in our hearts cannot be found by looking "outside." A line quoted by Wu-men, a thirteenth-century Chinese Zen Master, in his famous collection of koans called the *Wumen-kuan* (Gateless Gate), notes that "nothing which enters through the gate can be a genuine family treasure." Thus, nothing that comes to us "from the outside" can ever be counted among our precious possessions. In other words, an heirloom that is cherished and passed on through the ages is that which has been handed down from our very own ancestors. And indeed our true treasure, what the New Testament calls the "pearl of great price," is what is hidden yet undiscovered in the field of our very self. Thus, we are called to dig it up and bring it (and ourselves) to light. That wholeness we are in search of comes from this foundation, that is, the discovery of the treasure that lies within us; and to get to that treasure requires that we delve into the depths of our own being—the only solid foundation upon which any real structure can be built. And to do so requires that we cut through all the pseudo-structures we have set up for ourselves, built as they are upon sand.

It is these pseudo-structures that haunt us with that feeling of hollowness and superficiality, that make us ill at ease with ourselves. This feeling is the one that the Second Ancestor of Chinese Zen discovered in himself at the beginning of his Zen career, and it led him to seek direction and become a disciple of Bodhidharma. A koan from *The Gateless Gate* (case 41) tells us of his search. The koan begins:

> "Teacher, my mind is not at peace. I entreat you, set
>   me at peace."
> Bodhidharma replies, "Bring your mind to me, and I will set it
>   at peace."
> "I have searched everywhere for the mind but have never been
>   able to find it."
> And Bodhidharma replies, "There, I have finished putting it at
>   peace for you."

Bodhidharma's first injunction is addressed to each one of us as well: We must each, with our own unique temperaments, earnestly search for true peace of mind. But what will we find?

Bodhidharma invites each of us first of all to look within, to look at the mind that is not at peace and to fathom it at its very source, by sitting intently in zazen. The practice of this koan thus involves that indefatigable search for one's own mind, the root of one's anxieties, plunging into the depths of one's being. Putting it simply, this is what we are doing in Zen sitting. In the course of this we are enabled to see in the proper light those things that we have falsely identified with our self and our self-image, our social position, our security blankets, our material or even spiritual possessions, our natural talents and gifts, as well as our shortcomings, and weaknesses—all those things associated with our "identity." We are able to recognize in a similar way those things that fill our mind "from the outside," that tend to divide us and set us into disparate elements. Through Zen sitting, we are able to see through these and realize that our core is not contaminated by "outside elements." No, the True Self, the very mind we are required to take possession of, cuts through these elements one by one, getting to the core. This is similar to the process of peeling an onion whereby we take off and let go of layer after layer until we get to...what? Such a process is what I refer to in speaking about Zen.

The process can be rather trying, as we are forced to confront the pseudo-structures we have built for ourselves and toward which we nurture great attachment. We are called to peel them off one by one, to empty ourselves of them. This will give us a sense of not having anything left to cling to as we eliminate those things that gave us a sure footing, and with which we felt secure. But the True Self is not this. As we deepen in this process, going from one negation to the next—"not this, not this"—what is left?

In the practice of koans such as the one with Bodhidharma above, the Zen teacher plays a valuable role in pointing out those pseudo-structures to us, as we bring things that we have falsely identified with the mind. "No, not this. Go and sit some more." This process takes a different amount of time or length of practice with each given individual. For some, it may take only a few weeks, and for others, several months. And for yet others, it may require years and years. But it is only after having undergone such a process that one will be able really to grasp and make one's own the truth of this koan.

The disciple comes up to the Bodhidharma and exclaims, "Teacher, I have undergone this process of searching for the mind. It cannot be found." Or in more familiar terms we might say, "I've done all I can and it hasn't worked, and now I'm exhausted. I give up!" And we raise our hands up in total surrender.

Bodhidharma's reply can then become a "turning word," a sudden trigger for a new realization. The moment arrives as the Bodhidharma's words resonate from our very depths, and we know precisely what he means when he addresses us, saying, "There, I have put your mind at peace."

Merely to read the koan and try to interpret its content intellectually, without having undergone this taxing process of searching, of mental grappling and emptying, is to miss its point. This koan is an invitation for us to enter this arduous process, the one we venture into every time we sit zazen, composing ourselves by folding our legs and straightening our backs, regulating our breathing, focusing our minds to the point of ripe concentration. We are called to become the disciple, in an earnest search for peace of mind, in this indefatigable striving to get to the bottom of that mind and take possession of it, to experience the unattainable. We are invited to surrender everything, even the search itself! It is there that the revelation of a whole new world, a whole new universe, is waiting for us.

This invitation is no less than the one extended by Jesus to the rich young man in search of eternal life: "Go and sell all that you have, give it to the poor, and come, follow me" (Luke 10:21).

Jesus thus calls on him to divest himself of all his cherished possessions, let them go and enter a hitherto totally unknown territory in following the Son of Man—an act of total emptying, prerequisite to the full reception of the eternal life he was seeking. And entering into this realm is like entering through the eye of a needle, whereby all our excess baggage and attachments, false self-images, notions of self-importance, discriminative thoughts, and so forth, are recognized for what they are: hindrances we must cast away in order to attain what we seek.

To sit in Zen requires that we let go of all our cherished possessions centered on the attachment to what we normally call the "self." We are called to undercut all the layers of this, to get to its very source and bring it to the Zen teacher, that we may be set at peace. But of course, it is not the teacher who sets us at peace. Rather, it is the very discovery of that unattainable mind, or of mind as unattainable, that is itself the source of peace. Or, to switch back to Christian language: Realizing this is eternal life.

But eternal life is not a mere extension of time that knows no end, or even a state of continued deathlessness. It is, rather, a realm that cuts through all our concepts of time, of birth and death, change and decay. It is a realm in which all our familiar concepts have fallen away, as all of them are limited by their opposites. In this realm such notions as time and eternity, permanence and change, stillness and motion, universality and particularity lose their force as antithetical pairs. In this realm, all opposites find their convergence, their coincidence, and concepts as such are emptied of content and canceled by their opposites. And such a coincidence (which is no mere coincidence!) is itself not a concept but an event, an experiencing of a realm that waits to be uncovered as we submit to the process of emptying.

The new world into which Jesus invites the wealthy young man, which is the Realm of Heaven itself, requires for its entry this total self-emptying that is at the same time a total self-giving, and an abandonment in trust. What is required of us is akin to the trust of Peter when he jumped out of the boat into the water at the beckoning of

Jesus—it is a step in trust, like this, that we are likewise called to take and that we yearn to take. It is only our own hesitations, our second thoughts and calculating frames of mind—all indicative of a lack of trust—that cause us to bog down and sink into the water, as Peter did, the moment he began to doubt the power that kept him afloat (Matthew 14: 28–31).

The Realm of Heaven that awaits us is always here, right before us. Complaining that one cannot see it is like complaining of thirst when one is in the midst of fresh water, as an analogy the eighteenth-century Zen master Hakuin brings out in has famous "Song of Zazen," and failing to see it is the condition of an heir of a rich family who gets lost and wanders about having forgotten his own family origins.

Scriptural references to the Realm of Heaven are thus always of an allusive and elusive nature. They invite us to discover for ourselves the actual Presence. "Lo, the Realm of Heaven is in your midst. Be transformed in mind and heart,† and accept the Good News!" (Mark 1:15). It is hidden and revealed at the same time. It is not an idea or concept, but a reality to be grasped, felt, tasted. "Those who have eyes to see, let them see. Those who have ears to hear, let them hear!" (Mark 4:9–12). But to do this requires a casting away entirely of discriminatory thoughts that separate the seer and the seen, the hearer and the heard. No eye hath seen, no ear hath heard, what God hath prepared for those who love! (1 Corinthians 2:9). And this total emptying is on this very same account a realization of fullness—in Christian terms, the fullness of the loving God permeating one's entire being.

Let us look at this from another angle. From the point of view of *enlightenment as process,* "emptying" becomes an apt expression, indicating movement, entrance into the Realm. From the point of view of *enlightenment as state of realization or attainment,* the term "emptiness" is most aptly employed. But a disadvantage of this latter term is that it can be easily taken as a mere philosophical notion that sidetracks us from the actual Zen experience.

---

† My own translation from the Greek of *metanoiete,* usually rendered as "repent," but which is literally a transformation of mind and heart, turning away from selfishness, toward God.

Indeed emptiness, considered by many scholars the central notion of Buddhist philosophy, is accompanied by a whole set of philosophical-metaphysical presuppositions, with implications for a particular outlook on the totality of reality. There are many insightful and thought-provoking books in Western languages dealing with this notion of emptiness (my favorite is Frederick Streng's *Emptiness: A Study in Religious Meaning*)—however, I am not talking of emptiness here in the mode of a philosophical discourse, but am using the term as a pointer to an experience. My Zen teacher's Zen teacher, Yasutani Roshi, frequently cited a verse to express this experience of emptiness: "A clear blue sky, not even a speck of cloud to mar the gazing eye."

These two points of view in the Realm—entrance into it as movement or process, and the *fact* of it as attained—are represented by the complementary stances of the two disciples of the Fifth Chinese Zen Ancestor, Hung-jen (601–674). The story goes that the aging Hung-jen asked his disciples to compose a stanza to show their inner states of enlightenment, so he could choose his successor from among them. The foremost disciple, Shen-hsiu (606–706), wrote:

> *The body is the Bodhi tree*
> *The mind is a clear mirror stand*
> *Strive to polish it always*
> *Letting no speck of dust to cling.*

It is said that all the other monks read this in admiration as quite expressive of the Zen path, and thus expected Shen-hsiu to be given the right of succession as the new teacher.

Seeing this verse, however, a scullery boy working at the Zen monastery at the time scribbled the following:

> *There is no Bodhi tree*
> *There is no clear mirror stand*
> *From the beginning not one thing is*
> *Where then can a speck of dust cling?*

Hung-jen marveled at this expression, and this scullery boy, who exhibited his state of enlightenment through the stanza as handed down in the story, was then secretly chosen as successor; he later became known as the Sixth Chinese Zen Patriarch, Hui-neng (638–713).

Although the two verses above are usually presented as a contrast, to emphasize the depth of insight of the second, displaying the limited perspective of the first, these can also be seen as complementary, giving us a fuller picture of the world of Zen.

The first stanza emphasizes the process whereby one maintains active vigilance in polishing the mirror of enlightenment, that is, the process of emptying as a continuing, ongoing event. The latter, on the other hand, emphasizes the state of being empty from the very start and looks at everything from this standpoint, a state of perfect tranquillity. Although each already implies the other, their juxtaposition as complementary emphases serves to balance the two elements of process and state.

Thus, the Realm is presented in scripture as calling for active vigilance, as in the parable of the ten virgins (Matthew 25:1–13). Here, everyone is enjoined to continue being alert, being attentive every moment, and to spare no effort in mindfulness. Yet, the Realm is also likened to someone who sowed seed and then went to sleep, with the seed growing forth on its own, independent of human effort (Mark 4:26–29). Active vigilance is enjoined, but at the same time, there is equal emphasis on that trusting stance of just letting the Realm be as it is, as the lilies of the field and the birds of the air (Matthew 6:26–28).

In the two verses above, the enlightened mind is likened to a perfectly clear mirror. But in this example there is no substantial entity that is called "mirror" as such, only what it reflects. And thus, the perfect clarity of the mirror, its total "emptiness," is precisely what gives it the capacity to contain the whole universe within it. The whole universe is perfectly contained in the perfectly clear mirror, as nothing stands in the way of things being fully reflected in it. Precisely because it is totally empty, it is totally full! Thus the fully enlightened mind, the fully emptied person, contains the universe in its fullness and totality, perfectly.

To understand better this likening of the fully emptied person to a perfectly clear mirror, a reference to the four characteristics of the wisdom of the mirrorlike, enlightened mind recounted in Buddhist texts is apt.

First, just as a fully polished, clear mirror is able to reflect everything totally, the mirrorlike enlightened mind is able to reflect the totality of the universe as it is. It is characterized by an *all-embracing*ness that knows no bounds. Everything in the universe, in fullness and totality, is reflected in the mirror of the enlightened, fully emptied mind. Nothing is excluded from the realm of its concern. Indeed, *only* the fully emptied mind is able to comprehend, with all the saints, what is the breadth and length and height and depth of that which surpasses all knowledge. Only the mind that is totally emptied can be totally "filled with all the divine fullness" (Ephesians 3:18–19). Second, the perfectly clear mirror reflects all things equally, not giving preference to something because it is beautiful as opposed to unsightly, large as opposed to small, colorful as opposed to drab. All things are reflected as they are. And so too the fully emptied person is able to accept all things and all persons as they are, in an equal way, without preference or prejudice. Nor will such a person hold riches higher than poverty, attractiveness above homeliness. He or she will simply take these for what they are, as they are, without judgment. In the Realm of Heaven there is no distinction between "Greek and Jew, circumcised and uncircumcised, Scythian, slave or free" (Colossians 3:11).

Third, the mirror nevertheless reflects each thing and each person in its uniqueness, in its particularity, in its *suchness*. Thus something unsightly is as such unsightly, something beautiful is as such beautiful, hot is hot, cold is cold, black is black, gray is gray. In other words, nothing loses its particularity and irreplaceable uniqueness. In the Realm of Heaven, though there is one body, the head is nevertheless the head, the ear is the ear, the eye is the eye—each is each uniquely what it is.

Fourth, the mirrorlike enlightened mind is able to reflect the universe appropriately in all circumstances. Fully emptied persons are able to give of themselves according to the particular demand that the situation presents. To someone hungry, they will provide food. To someone naked, they will offer clothing. To someone sick or lonely or downcast, they will be there for healing, to give solace, companionship, hope. In short, enlightened persons are totally available and able to respond to each situation, able to be "all things to everyone" in the manner of Paul: "To the Jews, I became a Jew...to those under the law, I became as one under the law...to those outside the law, I became as one outside the law; to the weak, I became weak.... I have become all things to everyone" (1 Corinthians 9:19–22). Such universal availability, the capacity of being all things to all, is only possible to fully emptied persons, offering themselves totally without a taint of self-seeking or utilitarian motivation. Such a person will be to others what they need him or her to be for them.

All-embracingness, acceptance of all in equality, recognition of each in its uniqueness, and universal availability and responsibility according to each one's needs—these are the four characteristics of the wisdom of the mirrorlike enlightened mind. This is the inner state of the person who experiences total emptying. Such a state, on the one hand, manifests full transparency, perfect tranquillity. On the other hand, it manifests the dynamic activity of everything reflected upon it—that never-ending activity of being born and aging and dying.

This is the experience Zen offers. It is therefore a misunderstanding to consider Zen an individualistic, self-centered practice or a solipsistic kind of spirituality. Such a misunderstanding is easily generated, even by those who practice Zen themselves, if they cut themselves off from the rest of society and its pressing problems. But that is a kind of spiritual luxury we cannot afford in a world filled with violence from all sides, facing tremendous socioeconomic and ecological crises, in a human society that continues to perpetrate various injustices in manifold ways—all this calls urgently for vigilant concern and active involvement for its betterment. We cannot retreat into a haven of serenity and isolation, in a secluded meditation hall where the cries of the rest of the world are snuffed out by the meanderings of our monkey mind, by the sounds of our own breathing, or by the repetitious recitation of Mu. Zen is not merely that.

On the contrary, Zen practice grounds a stance that is attentive and sensitive to the pains of the world, empowering a person to plunge himself or herself in the tasks of transforming the world toward the alleviation of pain and suffering. This is a socially engaged Buddhism, a spirituality of commitment to and passion for the world.

If the Zen practitioner isolates himself or herself for a time in order to sit in stillness and find peace of mind, it is to look for his or her True Self, the discovery of which is the discovery of the real and deep bond that makes that person one with society, with the marketplace, with the whole universe.

Above I referred to the process of letting go of one's attachments, false self-images, prejudices, and discriminating thoughts, and of attaining that state of the "clear blue sky with no speck of cloud to mar the gazing eye," which is central in Zen. Under this clear blue sky everything comes into right focus—the beauty of a rose, the smell of jasmine, the taste of porridge as well as the ache in one's legs, the noise of the speeding taxi, the dust on the road. But also, the refugees, the political prisoners, the starving children. Here one's True Self comes to the fore, in and through these things that make up the warp and woof of our daily existence. It is not something distinct from these mundane realities. One is able to recognize one's True Self in the voices of a street vendor, in the homeless person seeking a handout on the city sidewalks, in the undocumented persons who provide us their services and yet are consigned to work for a pittance, but also in the executive caught in the rat race of the corporate world, with no time to look at himself or herself and ask what it is all about. And in this recognition of one's True Self, one identifies with the joys as well as the pains of the world as one's very own.

One who is fully emptied in Zen finds himself or herself in everything, literally, and is able to identify fully with everything, to be all things, and thus to act in total freedom, according to what the particular situation demands. Such a one is no longer separated by the illusory barrier between himself and the "other." One sees one's True Self in the "other," the "other" in one's True Self.

The temporary isolation therefore that we choose in sitting in a quiet room or meditation hall ultimately leads to a re-connection. Sitting practice opens us to the discovery of our intimate relationship with every being, not as an abstract principle or philosophical concept, but as a concrete, experiential event that comes to the fore with every movement, every gaze, every word, every touch. We may choose such a period of isolation to meditate or sit in Zen, in order to see through ourselves, to enable us to empty ourselves of every-thing that serves as a hindrance to this discovery, that is, of our oneness and solidarity with everything that is. To realize this total emptying is to come to the realization of the infinite fullness in which we are one with the entire universe.

My teacher Yamada Roshi used to express this infinite fullness in emptying with a fraction that has zero for its denominator, as in $1/0$, or $2/0$, or $1000/0$. The numerator in its unique particularity as a given sum, is nothing other than you and I, this tree or that cat, this moun-tain, that river, each concrete thing in the phenomenal world. The denominator expresses that point wherein emptiness is realized, True Self reached in total self-emptying. We might ask how many times one can be divided by zero, and we might answer "it cannot be." Yet on the other hand, another answer might be, "an infinite number of times." Thus $1/0$ equals infinity as does $2/0$ or $1000/0$ or $1,000,00/0$. This zero-point is grasped in the unique particularity of each numerator, each phenomenon, every being. And from the standpoint of this *concrete infinity* (a conceptual absurdity), everything said above concerning the mirror begins to make sense.

And here we can return to *creatio ex nihilo,* "creation out of noth-ing." Rather than taking it as a philosophical doctrine, we can take it as an invitation to that experience of the nothingness that is at the heart of our being, that becomes the fulcrum for experiencing the infinite life of God pulsing through this being, through the universe, from moment to moment.

This experience of infinity in us, which is also the experience of our *no-thing*ness, propels us to the concrete uniqueness that is our self, putting our feet back to touch the ground, or better, our poste-rior on the sitting cushion and from there to the concreteness of our standing and walking, laughing and crying, eating and drinking, working and playing. Each is a complete and perfect manifestation of the Infinite.

The "ultimate reality" attained in Zen, then, is nothing separate from each and every thing we do, or are, in our everyday life, in the concrete. This is illustrated very well by the koan in which a monk approaches Chao-chou (the monk of *mu*-koan fame) and says, "I have just entered the monastery. Please instruct me in the essence of Zen." To this Chao-chou asks in return, "Have you had your breakfast?" The monk answers, "Yes, I have," whereupon Chao-chou tells him "Then wash your bowls." And at this, the monk attains a flash of insight into the essence of Zen (*Wumen-kuan,* case 7).

The "insight" attained by the monk in this case is not some abstruse philosophical truth about Zen, or even some profound Zen doctrine interpreting the "meaning" of Chao-chou's words. It is this concrete fact of his having taken breakfast and washed his bowls.

On the nature of this insight, Wu-men's poem exclaims:

Because it is so very clear
It takes longer to arrive at the realization.
If you know at an instant that candlelight is fire
The meal has long been cooked.

Indeed it *is* so very clear, clearer than the blue sky. Yet, to use some more "dirty" language to becloud the issue, it is to become full, in realizing one's True Self as one with the whole universe. Or again it is to empty oneself of such ideas or thoughts of realization and self, and universe, and to simply be oneself, one's True Self, in the daily tasks of living, rising, taking breakfast, washing up, going to work, getting tired, resting a bit, meeting friends, saying goodbye, getting sick, growing old, dying. Yet this is not a conception of rising, taking breakfast, washing, and so on, but *just that,* doing, replete with a fullness that excludes nothing—a *wholeness,* wherein one's whole being is in that act of rising, or taking breakfast, washing, or whatever. Each activity or passivity is, in being totally empty, fully and perfectly a manifestation of the True Self.

And so the ultimate fruit of Zen is nothing more, and nothing less, than becoming truly what one is: truly human, whole, at peace, at one with everything, yet emptied of everything. Such an ultimate goal is not outside the reach of anyone; the Realm of God is at hand, in our midst. "Those who have eyes to see, let them see." But to be able to see requires that total change of heart, a *metanoia* (Mark 1:15), that total emptying of self that makes for its true fullness in the light of God's grace. Zen Master Dogen's famous line on the Way of the Enlightened points to this very experience: "To attain the Way of the Enlightened is to attain one's True Self. To attain one's True Self is to forget oneself. To forget oneself is to be enlightened by the myriad things of the universe."

The great death of self is the birth to the newness of life, wherein birth and death will be no more: "Neither shall there be mourning nor crying nor pain, for the former things have passed away" (Revelations 21:4). And what remains? "A new heaven and a new earth" (Revelations 21:1), transparent in the clear blue sky, in which everything is "filled with all the fullness of God" (Ephesians 3:19). But these are mere words, hollow, clanging cymbals, unless one actually, bodily goes though that experiential path of total self-emptying in which lies this fullness. Zen opens this experiential path to anyone who cares to tread it.

The Heart Sutra
on Liberating Wisdom

ZEN HALLS AND TEMPLES in Japan often resound with the chanting of the Heart Sutra, a well-known piece of Buddhist scripture, highly regarded throughout the ages as a succinct expression of the essence of enlightenment. However, it must not be forgotten that Zen does not rely on verbal or conceptual expressions for the transmission of the living wisdom of enlightenment. Words and concepts are in Zen like a finger pointing to the moon. It would indeed be foolish to be so enthralled with the finger—gazing at it, analyzing it from various angles, making comparisons with other fingers—that one never notices the moon in its resplendent brilliance. Let us then look at the Heart Sutra as a finger that points to the moon. Look, how radiant!

The "heart" that the Sutra is concerned with is the heart of the Great Matter, *prajna-paramita,* which I translate freely as "liberating wisdom." *Paramita* means the "highest, perfect, supreme." It also means "gone beyond (to the other shore)," "transcendent," characterizing the wisdom *(prajna)* of one who has attained liberation from "this shore," this world of conflict and suffering. However, it must be stressed that this liberating wisdom *does not make one cease to be in the midst of this world of suffering and conflict.* In "attaining" that wisdom, one does not thereby cease to be a human being who continues to face the ordinary (and extraordinary) struggles that are part and parcel of humanity's lot.

Rather, the person who has come to this liberating wisdom finds perfect peace and freedom right in the midst of this life. This does not mean that he or she relishes the suffering or conflict, or that he or she has simply taken a passive stance that tolerates it, doing nothing to prevent or stop it. Liberating wisdom enables the enlightened person to transcend all opposites such as suffering versus comfort, conflict versus harmony, good versus evil, life versus death, this world versus the other world. Liberating wisdom fully accepts each situation each moment in its eternal fullness—be it in sickness or health, riches or poverty, success or failure, life or death—and as such, overcomes these oppositions. It is perfect freedom in perfect acceptance.

Liberating wisdom brings peace with the whole universe, one becomes unified with all that is, truly free, truly happy, truly human. It is the fount of genuine compassion whereby one's heart embraces all, where one is united with all living beings in their joys and sufferings, struggles and hopes. This wisdom lies latent in all of us, and its awakening will enable us to realize our life in its infinite fullness, in every particularity, as one awakens in the morning, takes breakfast, goes to work, relaxes, chats with friends, wipes off one's sweat, laughs, cries, sits, stands, falls asleep. In this wisdom, one is perfectly free, perfectly being what one is, just as one is.

Let us now take a look at the Heart Sutra's account of this wisdom.

> Avalokiteshvara Bodhisattva, practicing deep Prajna-paramita
> perceived the emptiness of all five conditions of existence and
> was thus freed of all suffering. O Shariputra, form is no other
> than emptiness, emptiness no other than form. Form is
> precisely emptiness, emptiness precisely form. Sensation,
> perception, impulses, and consciousness are also like this.

O Shariputra, all things are manifestations of emptiness. No one is born, no one dies. Nothing is impure, nothing pure. Nothing increases, nothing decreases.

Therefore, O Shariputra, in emptiness there is no form, sensation, perception, impulses, or consciousness. No eye, ear, nose, tongue, body, mind. No color, sound, smell, taste, touch, thought. No realm of sight, up to no realm of consciousness. No ignorance, no cessation of ignorance. No old age and death nor cessation of old age and death. No suffering, no cause or end to suffering, no path to end suffering. No wisdom, and no gain. No gain, thus Bodhisattvas live this Prajna-paramita and attain no hindrance of mind. No hindrance, therefore no fear.

Far beyond all delusion, nirvana is already here. All past, present and future Buddhas live this Prajna-paramita and attain supreme, perfect enlightenment. Thus, know that this Prajna-paramita is the holy mantra, the luminous mantra, the supreme mantra, the incomparable mantra by which all suffering is swept away. This is no other than Truth. Set forth this Prajna-paramita mantra and proclaim: Gaté, Gaté, Paragaté. Parasamgaté. Bodhi svaha. Heart of the Perfection of Wisdom Sutra.

THE BODHISATTVA AVALOKITESHVARA

The sutra opens with Bodhisattva Avalokiteshvara (*Kuan-Yin* in Chinese) in the practice of the profound *prajna-paramita,* going on to describe what he/she (for this being is often androgynous) perceives in this practice.

First of all, the term *bodhisattva* (literally, "wisdom-seeking being") refers to one in active search for this liberating wisdom. It was applied first to Gautama himself, the historical Buddha, referring primarily to him during the six-year period of religious search and discipline he underwent before attaining supreme enlightenment. In undertaking this search, he left a life of ease and security at the royal palace and immersed himself directly in the mystery of human suffering.

The term later took on other nuances, a prominent one being the seeker-after-wisdom who, in the final stage of the search just before entering *nirvana* chooses to remain "here" for a while in order to help and guide other living beings to their own liberation. The name Avalokiteshvara means one who perceives (hears and sees) the cries of suffering of all living beings in an unhampered way. In the Japanese rendering, this is Kanzeon or Kannon, and has come down in feminized form as a goddess who hears the cries of distress of all suffering beings. She is portrayed as having a thousand hands and eleven faces, signifying her ability to see in all directions, bridging all distances, and to extend whatever form of assistance each suffering being needs in his or her particular situation.

This readiness to hear the cries of the suffering of others and to extend a hand of assistance in their direction is thus to be understood likewise as the inner attitude of every seeker-after-wisdom. Such an inner attitude is further expressed in the fourfold vow of the bodhisattva, likewise recited regularly in Zen halls all over Japan and elsewhere:

> *Sentient beings are numberless; I vow to free them.*
> *Delusions are inexhaustible; I vow to end them.*
> *Gates to the Truth are countless; I vow to open them.*
> *The Enlightened Way is unsurpassable; I vow to embody it.*

By this vow, the bodhisattva embraces the whole universe, opens his or her heart to all beings in their service, and sets out to accomplish the impossible and reach the unreachable. Thus the search after true wisdom clearly does *not* involve a self-centered kind of religious discipline whereby one closes off the world and other people from one's concerns to lead a life of escape, seeking only one's own peace of mind, avoiding involvement with a troublesome world and troublesome people. One sits in *zazen* not as an isolated individual, but as one who bears the weight of the whole universe, as one who has embraced all living beings.

To give an interesting example of a bodhisattva, let me mention Kenji Miyazawa (1896–1933), a devout Buddhist who spent the latter part of his short life living and working among poor farmers in northern Japan. His inner attitude is summed up in his short poem entitled *"Ame ni mo Makezu"* (Undaunted by the Rain), a part of which goes as follows:

If in the East a sick child be,
rush to its bedside, attend to its need.
If in the West a weary mother be,
go, carry her bundle of grain for her.
If in the South a dying man should lie,
go and comfort him, saying "Fear not."
If in the North a quarrel ensues,
go and say "Stop such foolishness."

These words reveal a readiness to be of service where needed, like the hands of Kannon, ready to be extended to anyone in need.

Another example of an unflagging religious search coupled with perfect openness in the service of others is the life of Simone Weil. Her diaries and journals, published after her death, reveal to us a heart as wide as the universe, having made her own the sufferings of all the unfortunate who have ever lived, having lived in her body the pain of all the afflicted.

The bodhisattva is seen in contrast to the complacent, unreflecting person who nonchalantly leads his or her life in the pursuits of the senses and in the gratification of selfish desires. The bodhisattva has begun to see the futility and emptiness of selfish pursuits and has begun the search for something deeper, something lasting, for a "treasure that will not rot and no thief can take away" (cf. Luke 12:33). And the bodhisattva realizes that it is precisely in giving one-self in the service of others that this treasure each one of us seeks from the depths of our heart can be manifested.

Again, the true search for liberating wisdom is not a way of abandonment that turns one's back on the real world, the world of conflict and suffering, but a way of *embracing acceptance* that plunges the seeker right into the midst of that world precisely in order to conquer it. In Christian terminology, the royal road to the Realm of Heaven is the "Way of the Cross," whereby one follows Jesus in embracing the reality of human suffering and in so doing accomplishes the salvation of the universe. The fact that the Heart Sutra sets forth the Bodhisattva Avalokiteshvara as the realizer of liberating wisdom, as the model of every seeker, is quite significant in this respect. The seeker must *become* Avalokiteshvara himself (herself), hearer of the cries of suffering of all living beings. Thus is the path of realization of liberating wisdom opened.

PERCEPTION OF EMPTINESS

Avalokiteshvara Bodhisattva, practicing deep Prajna-paramita, perceived the emptiness of the five conditions of existence.

In the Buddhist conceptual framework, human existence is analyzed by way of a set of five constituents, namely, (1) matter or physical substance, or "form," (2) sensation, (3) perception, (4) impulses, or our reactions to stimuli, and (5) consciousness. We shall not trouble ourselves with an explanation of these categories, but shall simply rephrase the statement of the Heart Sutra: Everything we consider constitutive of our existence (in whatever way the elements are conceived to be, upon detailed analysis) is "empty."

The first temptation is to wax profound in a philosophical interpretation of this statement, which is rather crucial for the understanding of the core doctrine of Mahayana Buddhism. However, we are not concerned with just an intellectual appreciation of Buddhist doctrine, but rather with the living realization of wisdom, which can shed light on the question of our own existence. And to be told that what basically constitutes our existence is "empty" is like having the rug pulled out from under our feet, overturning whatever common sense we have about the substantiality of this existence of ours. In short, this statement of the Heart Sutra presents a challenge to our common sense and accepted ways of thinking, introducing a contradiction in our assumptions, like a sharp sword that lunges directly at one's heart, cutting right through one's most cherished conceptions. We are told that whatever we consider "of substance" is in fact empty, that is, "devoid of substance."

A mind-boggling proposition indeed: "*A* is not *A*." This is not unlike the famous *mu*-koan in which to the question, "Does a dog have Buddha-nature?" Chao-chou answers, *"Mu!"* And now the practitioner is asked by the teacher, "What is *mu?* Show me *mu!"* As a practitioner goes forth to present one answer after another, she is told, time and again, "No, not this!" After a while, she is driven into a corner, having exhausted all conceivable answers. Then her conceptual thinking comes to a full stop as she faces a blank wall. It is only in this full stop, this *zero-point* of conceptual thinking, that there can burst forth the liberating power of *mu,* unleashing all the energy of the whole universe, re-creating everything anew.

And it is only from this zero-point that one can grasp the full import of the term "emptiness," that is, after one has actually gone through the process that leads to experiencing it. Hence there is no use in expounding on a theory of "the meaning of emptiness" and the like, as it will only offer another conceptual alley to get trapped in. The seeker now must gear himself or herself toward that full stop, and "empty" himself or herself of everything that comes in the way. How is this to be accomplished?

The way consists in divesting oneself of everything, as I have said earlier. And now the Heart Sutra offers an additional hint in this process: It urges the throwing away of that view of our existence as "substantial," in other words, that clinging to what we may call the "phenomenal self" or "ego," the root of all selfishness and avarice and envy and lust and what-have-you. It is this clinging that sets a human being in conflict with another, that alienates a person from others, from nature, from his or her own True Self; this is what must be emptied.

It is my clinging to this phenomenal self that makes me want this car, that house, more money, the admiration of others, the power to influence people's lives, a name to be remembered in history. My pursuit of these things sets me in conflict with others who are also after them. Here we have Juan and Pedro each wanting a larger and larger share of cake, being at odds with one another, Juan grabbing Pedro's share, Pedro getting even through physical violence, Juan retaliating, and so on—the world of opposition and conflict and mutual exploitation among human beings, as self-interests are set against those of others. On a global scale we have ethnic group against ethnic group, nation against nation, rich nation exploiting poor nation, poor nations seeking to get the better of each other, resulting in mutual resentment and often physical violence and warfare. A bird's-eye view of the world today presents such a picture of conflict everywhere, and this is nothing but the result of that attachment to the phenomenal self that is deeply rooted in each individual.

The right understanding of what the Heart Sutra means by "emptiness," then, involves the letting go of this phenomenal self or ego, a total emptying, which is no less than a complete abandonment of all of one's cherished possessions—not unlike the call received by the rich young man who was in search of eternal life.

> As Jesus was setting out on a journey, a man ran up before him, asking, "Good Teacher, what must I do to attain eternal life?"…"You know the commandments: do not kill, do not commit adultery, do not steal, do not bear false witness, do not defraud others, honor your father and mother." And he said to him, "Teacher, I have observed all these from my youth." And Jesus, looking at him, loved him, and said to him: "You lack one thing. Go and sell what you have, give to the poor, and you will have treasure in heaven. And come, follow me." But at this the man's face fell, and he went away sad. For he had many possessions. (Mark 10:17–23)

So the central statement of the Heart Sutra that "the five conditions of existence are empty" is the fundamental *negation* not only of our whole conceptual apparatus, whether we think in line with the Buddhist conceptual framework or not, but of our entire ego-centered existence. This negation is thus an injunction to divest ourselves of such a mode of existence. It is a call from a self-centered life, unreflective, engaged only in the pursuits of the senses and in the gratification of selfish desires, to a life lived in the search for and discovery of an eternal treasure, a life lived in the service of that liberating wisdom that opens the heart to others, the call to walk the path of the bodhisattva. A life of self-centeredness, a life lived in the pursuit of the desires of the phenomenal ego, can only end in frustration and futility. Such a life is like a structure built upon sand, a structure bound to crumble from the very start.

And where is the secure foundation for the new edifice to be found? Where is the fount of that lasting treasure, the locus of that liberating wisdom? It is on the experiential arrival at *zero-point* mentioned above, whereby one grasps indeed that *all is emptiness, and emptiness is all!* A clear blue sky, with no trace of cloud to mar the gazing eye.

Experiencing this, one is opened into an entirely new world, and yet nothing changes of the old: Mountains are high, valleys are low, roses are red. And yet again, all this is seen in an entirely new light: Each of these particularities is a full and perfect manifestation of that world of emptiness, each action and passion replete with a fullness of its own, each moment an eternity.

That experiential zero-point is the fulcrum on which is based the liberating wisdom of which the Heart Sutra speaks. And at this point all opposites are reconciled, as the universe of concepts gives way to the universe of living experience.

NEGATION OF CONCEPTS, INVITATION TO EXPERIENCE
O Shariputra, all things are manifestations of emptiness. No one is born, no one dies. Nothing is impure, nothing pure. Nothing increases, nothing decreases.

We are faced here with more conceptual contradictions, and our commonsense understanding of things must necessarily be shattered. How are we, for example, to reconcile the above negations with the everyday facts that babies are born, people die, things get dirty and are cleaned the population increases while the food supply decreases, and so on?

Here is the secret: *There is simply no way to reconcile these contradictions in our heads.* It is just that if everything can be seen *just as it is,* without any concepts of "arising" or "annihilation," of "impurity" or "increase," then we can see indeed that there is no arising nor annihilation, no purity or impurity, no increase or decrease. A baby is born, and cries "Waaa!" *Just that.* A good friend dies unexpectedly. *Just that.* Oops, that passing car splashed all this mud all over my white shirt and trousers. *Just that.* Ah, a single wash with soap brings back the whiteness. *Just that.*

We can now get a hint as to the next string of negations that the Heart Sutra confronts us with. The five constituents of existence (mentioned above) are negated. And so are the organs of sense, their respective object-fields, and the various sensations that result from their functioning. And likewise the twelve links in the chain of causation, beginning with "ignorance" and ending with "old age and death," together with the Four Noble Truths themselves, and finally, the very fact of enlightenment. In other words, all the basic teachings of Buddhism are here negated.

This may seem tantamount to Buddhist blasphemy, denying outright what has been traditionally revered as the teaching of the Buddha, perhaps akin to a Christian denying the doctrines of the Apostle's Creed point by point. I am reminded of another "blasphemy," frequently repeated in Zen, whereby one is enjoined, "If you meet the Buddha, slay him!" One is tempted to say to the Christians, "If you meet the Christ, crucify him!"

Such injunctions are indeed jarring, even shocking, but they are advisedly and purposefully so. For "doctrines" and "holy images" can become just an additional set of encumbrances that prevent one from the direct realization of what they were originally meant to convey.

Buddhism itself began with a powerful religious experience—that momentous experience of enlightenment of Gautama, which totally altered his outlook and his whole personality. It was a dynamic experience that continued to inspire his whole career and affected those who came in contact with him directly or indirectly. Buddhist doctrines came to be formulated mainly as attempts to verbalize, conceptualize, and systematize that experience (a futile attempt from the start!) for the purpose of transmission to others (an impossibility!). But the mastery of the verbalized, conceptualized, systematized teaching does not necessarily accompany the grasp of the essential point, which is the experience of that enlightenment, the fount of liberating wisdom. On the contrary, such verbalization, conceptualization and systematization often can positively hamper this liberating wisdom from coming to the fore.

The function of doctrines in Buddhism has frequently been likened to that of a raft: It can indeed be useful in carrying one over the waters, but to continue to carry the raft after getting ashore would be to shoulder a useless burden. But here in the Heart Sutra the raft is abandoned in midstream; it is the only way to discover that what one is looking for, what one is aiming at right from the start, is right here in the midst of the water!

Thus the injunction to kill the Buddha if one meets him along the road is the command to do away with one's mental images of the Buddha, as well as to do away with the opposition of "Buddha" and "non-Buddha" or "ordinary being." With the image thus eliminated, the real thing comes to the fore, and then one is able to see everything with the eyes of the Buddha himself, with the eye of nondiscrimination that has transcended all such opposition.

The parallel injunction to the Christian about "crucifying Christ" may have a different ring, but its purport is the same—to clear away all our pious images of Christ and thus "put him in his place," which is on the cross, where he is one with all beings in their suffering, where he is reduced to nothing in total emptying *(kenosis)*. "Christ Jesus, who though he was the form of God, was not attached to this equality with God, but emptied himself, taking the form of a servant, being born in the likeness of a human being. And being found in human form, he humbled himself, becoming obedient unto death, even to death on a cross" (Philippians 2:7–9). It is this total emptying on the cross that leads to the bursting forth of the new life of the resurrection, and the outpouring of the Breath of God, that marked the salvation of the whole universe. And for the Christian, this is not merely a past event that happened some two thousand years ago to some wandering Galilean, but it is a present reality here and now. The basis of the Christian life is this cross and resurrection, total self-emptying and total newness of life. Our intention here is not to make a theological statement, but to heed the invitation to a direct experience of a present reality. "It is no longer I that live, but Christ in me" (Galatians 2:20); here is Christ crucified and resurrected in the newness of life, empowered with full authority in the whole universe.

The negation of doctrines and concepts is neither agnosticism nor intellectual irresponsibility and anarchy, but an invitation to experience the reality that underlies the doctrines and concepts.

To give another example, the denial of God's existence is usually interpreted as the acceptance of an atheistic worldview. But this is itself the setting up of the opposite *doctrine* of God's nonexistence. Liberating wisdom would reject both, and instead present the invitation to experience the reality of "God" as manifested in each present moment. It is the invitation to see everything in the very eyes of God, as is—blasphemy of blasphemies, yet wonder of wonders: "Everything is filled with the fullness of God!" (Ephesians 3:19). But again, let this not be mistaken for pantheism, the doctrine that *equates* everything with God. We are not talking of *doctrine* here, but simply of an invitation to hear with the ears and see with the eyes of the heart. "Blessed are the pure of heart, for they shall see God" (Matthew 5:8). This is the vision available only from the perspective of liberating wisdom. A clear blue sky, without a trace of cloud to mar the gazing eye!

THE TRUTH OF SUFFERING

Among the Buddhist doctrines the Heart Sutra sets up for negation are the Four Noble Truths: the Truth of Suffering, and the accompanying Truths of the Cause of Suffering, the Cessation of Suffering, and the Path to the Cessation of Suffering. The Truth of Suffering expresses a rather fundamental feature of our human existence, and its negation in the Heart Sutra again forces us against a wall.

Gautama embarked on his religious journey in quest of the key to the mystery of human suffering. Jesus crowned his short earthly career by fully accepting intense suffering and an ignominious death upon the cross. Suffering is a blatant fact we encounter, in varying degrees of intensity, in our day-to-day life. Even a casual glance at the media, or a surface awareness of the situation of the world today, puts one face-to-face with this fact. Hundreds of thousands throughout the world live on the brink of starvation and in constant threat of death. Numberless refugees have been displaced from places they can call home, due to political, socioeconomic, and other factors. In Asia, Africa, and Latin America, millions are deprived of even the bare necessities of human existence due to flagrantly unjust social structures. Industrial laborers in various countries are constantly plagued by oppressive working conditions and unfair labor practices, treated as mere tools of profit rather than as human persons. Countless individuals and groups throughout the world are discriminated against or persecuted for their race, religion, skin color, sex, political convictions, and so on. It is indeed an endless list.

The underlying presupposition in all this is that suffering is an undesirable element that humanity strives to eradicate from its existence with all the means at its disposal, and that the picture of an ideal existence would be one freed from such suffering. Hence, we tend to make distinctions between this world of suffering, this "vale of tears," and the "other world," "the other shore" where all such suffering has ceased, where all is bliss, whether it be the Buddhist *nirvana,* the Christian heaven, or some form of earthly utopia. The attainment of such a state is the hope that springs eternal in the human heart.

How then are we to take the negation of the Truth of Suffering in the Heart Sutra, which states that "there is no suffering, no cause, no cessation, no path to end suffering"? What does this mean to the father of the family of eight whose shanty has just been demolished by government troopers to make way for the construction of a hotel and tourist center? Or to a young couple who have heard from the doctor that their first child of less than one year is dying of a skin disease aggravated by malnutrition? Or to a political detainee who is subjected to interrogation and physical abuse at the hands of the military, deprived of needed sleep, food, and drink?

A glimpse of an answer came to me years ago during a meeting with a group of farmers and their families in a barrio in the northern part of the Philippines, during the period of its history under the Marcos dictatorship. A few weeks previous to that meeting, ten of their companions had been picked up by military troopers and, after being abused and tortured, were sent home, except for three, whose bodies were found burnt to the bone upon exhumation from a common grave in the cemetery of the next town. And now the bereaved families and some sympathetic friends were gathered together at this meeting, reporting further developments and consulting with each other as to what steps to take. It seemed that the harassment by the military would keep on, as they would come to the farmers' homes fully armed in search of certain family members who in turn were forced to go into hiding; in the meantime the soldiers would prey on whatever they found available——chickens, livestock, and so forth.

It would be too complicated to describe fully the background of the situation, but this group of farmers and their families were being forced to the edge of a cliff. Should they turn in the family members who were being sought by the authorities? Some of these were girls in their teens, and their fate could well be imagined if they were to fall into the hands of the soldiers. The people knew if they kept on refusing and maintained them in hiding that there would be no end to this present harassment. In the meantime they could not go back to work on their farms as long as this situation continued, and thus their very source of life was being threatened. In other words, given the alternatives, there was no conceivable way out for them. They were faced with a living koan, a koan with the weight of life and death.

This living koan is precisely what led them to the *zero-point*. And what happened at that meeting I was privileged to attend was a communal experience of the *zero-point*. Their lives had been emptied of all possible human hope, and they had, literally, nothing more to lose. And it was in this situation, emptied of everything, that everyone felt a new freedom, a new light. The way one of them expressed it to me was, "God is with us. We have nothing to fear!" And this expression uttered right then was not a mere "hope" or "faith" but an *experienced reality* that showed itself in the serenity of their faces, in the lightheartedness and sense of freedom that came at that very moment. "God is with us. There is nothing to fear!"

My description does no justice to the actual experience of the meeting itself, of a group placed in the very midst of physical and mental anguish and persecution, facing basic dilemmas in which there was no conceivable way out, accepting themselves and the situation as they were, and experiencing something that liberated them from such suffering *while being right in the midst of it*——a human experience of something close to pure joy and freedom and peace, right in the face of their contraries. *Zero-point*.

I do not know what happened to the members of the group afterward. Some more may have been picked up by the military, perhaps even killed. I do not know what the future held for those who were with us in that circle that day. All I know is that whatever happened afterward, the utterance that came forth from the communal experience of *zero-point* continues to ring true in my own being as an ever-present reality: "God is with us. There is nothing to fear!"

We need not be bogged down by attempts to "analyze" or interpret this expression, asking for definitions, challenging the meaning of the terms involved, like, "God," for example—a problematic term from many angles. (But see chapter 9, Zen Experience of Triune Mystery, for an attempt at addressing this question.) For the villagers, it came spontaneously from a deeply felt Christian conviction shared by the members of that group. We are invited simply to open our inner eye to see what they "saw" from within, from *zero-point*. It is from this same *zero-point* that the Heart Sutra exclaims, "There is no suffering, no cause of suffering, no cessation of suffering, no path to the cessation of suffering."

NO WISDOM, NO ATTAINMENT

Another puzzling statement of the Heart Sutra appears, which seems to subvert everything the very Sutra stands for: "There is no wisdom, no attainment." We are again placed in apparent self-contradiction, after all this talk of liberating wisdom and the ways to its attainment.

Let us recall, however, that this is uttered from the standpoint of that wisdom itself, shining in splendor as full as the noonday light. On a bright, clear and cloudless day, the pure white light of the sun illuminates all things just as they are. It is the pure white light that enables everything to be seen, yet it itself does not come within vision. In the same way, liberating wisdom, while enlightening all things and enabling everything to be seen as it is, itself does not come within the field of vision; it is oblivious of its own existence!

This is what makes for the total freedom and detachment of liberating wisdom. It betrays no self-consciousness that sets up an opposition between itself as "wise" and something else as "foolish." This obliviousness and total absence of self-consciousness is what makes the person matured in liberating wisdom hard to notice in a crowd. There is no sheen, no glare, no flashy element that would attract attention to itself.

In Zen one who comes to a certain experience of enlightenment sees an entirely new world for the first time, and for a time remains in the thrall of the novelty, the wonderment, the brilliance of this new perspective. In this immediate stage after that experience a certain glare remains, a certain consciousness that goes with the powerful emotions that the experience may have triggered. A tinge of attachment to the enlightenment experience remains, understandably, because it is something very intimate, very precious, something that has definitely affected one's entire outlook on life and on the universe. But if this gets out of hand, it easily leads to what is known as "Zen sickness," overenthusiasm with Zen-like expressions and paraphernalia, coupled with an extranormal propensity to bring Zen into normal conversations even when uncalled for, an overzealousness to "convert" others to Zen. Or perhaps worse, one unwittingly succumbs to the temptation of pride, because one has had an experience that others have not, and in unsubtle ways, one begins to flaunt that fact.

But such a pitfall is alien to genuinely matured liberating wisdom. It is the task of post-enlightenment practice, with the help of koans that serve this purpose, to grind away this sheen, to sweep away this self-conscious attachment to the experience. This is meant to enable the practitioner to become his or her normal self again, reacting as a normal being in all things, seeking food when hungry, rest when tired, heat when cold, feeling indignation against injustice, compassion for the suffering of others. And yet again with a difference. In each of these events and encounters in daily life, the person is at peace with his or her True Self, one with the entire universe. Each event, each encounter exhausts one's total self, and there remains an infinity to give. Each moment is a complete realization of the True Self in each concrete situation. But in all this, there is no need to think twice and say, "In this act I am one with the universe." One is simply so, and that is all.

In the same way as liberating wisdom is oblivious of its own existence, so too is true compassion, which springs from it and is characterized by the total absence of self-consciousness. The truly compassionate person spontaneously becomes one with another in suffering. He or she does not have to pause and say, "Ah, what a pity!" as if from the standpoint of one outside the pain. One is spontaneously able to make that pain one's very own, and thus respond accordingly from *within* the pain itself. A mother in the midst of caring for her sick child does not have to say, "Ah, poor child." For the pain of the child is her very own pain, and she feels the pain perhaps even more than the child itself and is entirely oblivious to her own discomfort in giving the child the care it needs in its sickness.

Thus true compassion does not count its "merits" and become complacent at having done a "good deed." For example, in the New Testament injunction to one who has two coats that he or she give to one who has none, the giver will have no room to say, "Ah, I did a good thing in giving that other coat of mine; I expect at least a sense of gratitude from the wretch!" For one has simply done what is most natural in the situation, as water would flow from a higher to a lower place, without the least feeling of condescension. In true compassion based on liberating wisdom, the left hand knows not what the right hand is doing (Matthew 6:3).

At this point I am reminded of the story of two Zen monks, a young man and his elder companion, riding on a crowded train on their way back to Kamakura after an errand in Tokyo. The young monk was intent to keep a posture becoming of a monk, careful and wary of the gaze of the other passengers. The elder one, on the other hand, looked weary and kept nodding his head in half-sleep while standing and holding the suspended leather strap for balance. When they reached the station, the young monk half-chided the elder, letting other people witness such a sluggish and lazy-looking old monk. At this the elder monk simply retorted, "I was tired and sleepy!"

If we are to "translate" what the elder monk said that gives the story its point, it is this: "Your self-consciousness of how others think of you is your attachment. Be your natural self, alone, or with others. When you are tired and sleepy, you are tired and sleepy!"

It is only when one is firmly grounded in liberating wisdom that one can truly, freely say, "There is no wisdom." From the same standpoint one can say, "There is no attainment." For what is there to attain for one who dwells at the highest of attainments? Or from another angle, liberating wisdom simply comes to the fore, as clouds of delusion that block the pure white light disappear. This is no attainment, but simply a coming to what has been there from the start. And as the clouds of delusion caused by our self-centered thinking fall off or thin out, the seeker is freed of all hindrance of mind, and hence of fear and anxiety. Having shed all delusive attachments, he or she has nothing more to lose, nothing more to gain. *One is simply as one is!* What peace of mind, what freedom, what exhilarating joy! This is nirvana, the highest enlightenment *(anuttara-samyak-sambodhi),* in which all the Buddhas of the past, present, and future dwell.

THE HEART SUTRA AS MANTRA

The last few lines of the Sutra extol its glories as a great, luminous, unsurpassed, and supreme mantra, and end with a Sanskrit formula of the mantra. This word "mantra" originally meant a phrase or formula to be kept in mind and recited repeatedly in order to set the mind of the religious practitioner at focus on one point. The meaning further developed as a formula with dynamic power able to effect the union of the reciter with all the power in the whole universe. Thus the recitation of the Heart Sutra itself is believed to effect the realization of enlightenment in the very recitation, in the way Christian sacraments are understood to have the power to effect what they intend, which is union with God, in their very enactment.

In the light of the above, seeing that the exposition of liberating wisdom is in some senses the be-all and end-all of the Heart Sutra, such belief is not entirely without grounds. The whole Heart Sutra itself, as we mentioned in the beginning, is like a finger that points us to the moon, shining in all its brilliance on a cloudless night. So the earnest recitation of Heart Sutra can become a trigger for that experience of enlightenment. But of course, despite what the last lines of the Heart Sutra seem to say, it does not have to be the Heart Sutra mantra. It can be the sound of a gong, the ticking of a clock, a sneeze, the smile of a friend. A dewdrop, a whisper, a gentle breeze. Look, how radiant!

Every Day Is
a Good Day

THE SIXTH ENTRY OF THE *Pi-yen-lu* or "Blue Cliff Record" collection of koans begins with a question posed by Master Yun-men: "I am not asking you about the previous fifteen days. Now say something about these latter fifteen days."

The concrete reference of the koan, first of all, is to the waxing moon (first fifteen days) and the waning moon (the latter fifteen days). The break-off point here is the full moon or the experience of *kensho* or self-realization. Thus, the "previous fifteen days" refer to the period before enlightenment, a period of searching and digging and delving and "Mu-ing," wherein one applies total effort to enable the True Self to come to full light.

The "latter fifteen days" begin with and presuppose the experience of enlightenment. That experience is the discovery of one's True Self as one with all, as being no different from each and every particularity in the whole universe. This is the experience of the "full moon" of one's life. Indeed, in this experience, replete with joy and peace and inner satisfaction, one sees the *concrete* meaning of one's existence, not as an intellectual idea, but as a down-to-earth *fact*. With this, one becomes fully at peace and at home with oneself and the whole universe, and one is content even in the face of death. For the enlightened person, and for that person alone, every day truly is a good day. The point of the koan *is* to show one's realization of this "good day." "Now let your servant depart in peace, because my eyes have seen your salvation." The words of the prophet Simeon in Luke 2:29–32 reflect this kind of joy and sense of fulfillment at having come to what one has awaited and longed for over a long and arduous period. I am reminded of other words that have somehow become a part of me: "And now my own joy is made complete" (John 3:30).

Though varying with each individual, this experience of the "full moon" is so fraught with emotional overtones and undertones that it can take time for the sheen and luster to settle. A misdirected step can afflict one with what is usually called "Zen sickness," in which one keeps referring to this experience out of context or keeps throwing around Zen terms and phrases in conversations, even when they are not called for. One can come close to being a Zen maniac, trying to convert everybody in sight to this "very wonderful thing." Indeed, Zen may have done wonders for one, but for the bystander or onlooker or unfortunate victim of Zen talk it may simply be a smack of the exotic. The Latin term for moon is *luna,* the root of the word *lunatic.*

A mere hairbreadth distance from this, however, is the healthy Zen path, which calls for further unflagging exercise in polishing and rounding off the rough edges. The *post-kensho* koan training is thus a vital element and can make for the subtle difference between a pathological and a healthy Zen mind.

If we go back to the moon analogy, we see that the latter fifteen days is in the direction of a return to total darkness of the "new moon." It is a period of shedding attachment to the *kensho* experience as such, culminating at that point wherein sheen and luster are no more, and one is completely lost in the midst of darkness, that is, in the naked reality of this concrete day-to-day existence. Of course, now there is a great difference, a crucial difference, from before the experience of the full moon. Now one is at peace, at home with oneself and with the totality of the universe, no longer worried about perpetuating one's name or honor or riches or self-image. One is simply *there,* with every breath, every cough, every step, every event, every encounter, to the full.

It is about these "latter fifteen days" that Master Yun-men is asking. And he himself answers his own question.

It is easy to mistake this answer and think that Master Yun-men means that things turn out just fine every day. Let us not be misled by the words here though. Master Yun-men is speaking from the depths of the world of emptiness, *de profundis,* out of the depths, and not talking about phenomenal events.

Resonant language is found in the Book of Genesis, when God created the waters and the earth and plants and animals and human beings: God looked over the whole universe of his creation, each and every thing in it, and saw that *it was very good.* A total and unconditional affirmation of each and every thing as it is.

Again, this expression is not dealing with phenomenal events, or with goodness or badness of things in the phenomenal world. It is this dichotomy in words that leads to such questions as, If God created everything and saw that it was very good, why are there so many evils in the world? Innocent babies dying of disease and starvation, innocent people brutally murdered or subjected to military harassment, small elite classes enriching themselves at the expense of the worsening poverty of the multitudes. And so on. Indeed, we live in a world full of contradictions, full of evil and suffering and injustice. Does Master Yun-men close his eyes to these realities?

No, *not at all.* In fact, if you work on this koan in the *dokusan* room and present a situation wherein every day is fine weather, things going smoothly, business growing, everybody happy, and so on, you will be sent back to look at the *real* world, to present an answer based on *that.*

To be able to utter "Every day is a good day," from the true standpoint of enlightenment, one must have a solid grasp of the world as it is, and not some imaginary utopian kind of world where it never rains and there is only sunshine, like Southern California.

Let us take a stark look at this world of ours to be able to grasp the true import of Master Yun-men's words.

Recently I received news about a former college classmate who was killed in a military skirmish in a rural area in the Philippines. He had been "underground" for many years, having lost all hope for change through conventional, legal, and political means. I remember back in college days how he had been an active student leader, full of hope, full of concern for his country and his people. A tragic end for someone who had given his life for Filipinos in the way his conscience dictated.

And he has not been the only one. Countless others lose their lives in a similar manner all over the world, as they give voice to the injustices being perpetrated in our society, in this world of ours today. Many of those who have taken action against the established order in their societies, whose key concern is to serve their fellow human beings and alleviate their suffering, standing up for their rights and helping them be treated in a decent way as human beings, find themselves branded subversives or terrorists, and have now either been arrested or subjected to continuing harassment.

At present, of the 6 billion inhabitants of our planet, more than 900 million are living in situations of absolute poverty and starvation, and are on the brink of death. It is estimated that every minute, twenty-seven persons die of starvation-linked causes on this earth of ours. At the very moment this is being read, in different places all over the world, such deaths are occurring one after another. Countless individuals will be deprived of their basic rights to live by a situation of injustice and an unbalanced distribution of the world's resources and means of production.

Another impending reality that causes concern for humankind now is the continuing destruction of our natural environment. The earth's natural resources are being depleted by rampant and thoughtless exploitation in order to support the luxurious consumer habits of those who have money and power, at the expense of those who do not. One indicator of the situation is that by the year 2020 practically every available rain forest resource in the Third World will have been depleted if the felling and destruction continues at the present rate. It is estimated that in Asia alone the forest area decreases by

1,800,000 hectares per year. And all this is not yet to speak of environmental destruction from other causes, such as pollution due to large-scale industrial projects, or from nuclear-caused radiation, all of which are growing on a global scale.

And still another impending concern is, of course, the militarization of our globe. We continue to create and store weapons of mass destruction. Weapons are continually being manufactured and sold to authoritarian and repressive regimes to check the rising voices of discontent among the people.

Such are the contradictions of our real world today. This situation reminds us of the Burning House Parable in the famous Mahayana scripture, the Lotus Sutra. The Buddha, depicted as the compassionate father of all beings, looks at the world situation and compares it to a house whose walls and posts are burning and are about to collapse. His children remain oblivious of this fact and continue to romp and play inside the house, unaware of the coming destruction.

This is the real world that we are called on stare in the face before we can go on to tackle Master Yun-men's koan.

But a hint into this koan is also given to us by an entry in the *Miscellaneous Koans after Kensho,* concerning the stone in the bottom of the Sea of Ise:

> *In the sea of Ise, ten thousand feet down, lies a single stone.*
> *I wish to pick up that stone without wetting my hands.*

Let me not dally with an explanation of this koan here (see chapter 9, Zen Experience of Triune Mystery, for further exposition of what this koan involves), but simply mention the continuing part of the koan, which tells us that *that* mysterious stone both "cannot get wet" and yet also "cannot get dry." These two apparent contradictory characteristics of *that* stone, which we can call the stone of our True Self, give us the hint for grasping Master Yun-men's "Every day is a good day." "Cannot get wet" means that there is absolutely no opposition in this world, no object to be made wet or subject to wet, or the other way around. There is no polarity between subject and object, being born and dying, happiness and sorrow, good and evil. "Cannot get dry" means that tears of compassion continuously flow in this concrete world where living beings are in a state of suffering. And both these characteristics of this "mysterious stone" describe the situation seen from the point of view of the world of emptiness as such.

I recall the words of a wise sage from India who said, "What you are, the world is." And to this we have to add, "What the world is, is what you are." This is to see things in a way that dissolves the opposition between ourselves and the "world." The "world" is "what we are." The world is not something outside of us, something that we view as mere bystanders, lamenting its sorrows and evils. No, what happens to the whole world as such is what happens to our very own True Selves. The sickness of the world is our very own sickness. This is the sickness of the bodhisattva; it is a sickness that is also the hope and salvation of all living beings. In Christian terms it is the reality of the cross of Christ, the bearer of the sufferings of the world.

Only one who has experienced this realm, as one with all the crucified of the world, can truly say with Master Yun-men, "Every day is a good day."

The Song
of Zazen

All sentient beings are originally Buddhas.
As in the case of water and ice,
There is no ice without water,
No Buddhas apart from sentient beings.
Not realizing that Truth is so close,
Beings seek it far away—alas!
It is like one who, while being in the midst of water,
Cries out for thirst.
It is like the child of a rich household
Who gets lost in a poor village.
The reason why beings transmigrate through the six realms
Is because they are lost in the darkness of ignorance.
Wandering about from darkness to darkness
How can they be freed from the cycle of birth and death?
As to the Zen samadhi of the Great Vehicle,
No amount of praise can exhaust its treasures.

The six ways to perfection, beginning with Giving,
Living a right life, and other good deeds,
Intoning the name of Buddha, Repentance, and so on,
All these come down to the merit of Zen sitting.
The merit of one single sitting in Zen
Erases countless sins of the past.
Where then are the evil ways that can mislead us?
The Pure Land cannot be far away.
Those who, even once, with a humble disposition
Are able to hear this truth, praise it, and faithfully adhere to it,
Will be endowed with innumerable merits.
But if you turn your gaze within
And attest to the truth of essential nature,
That self-nature that is no-nature,
You will have gone beyond mere sophistry.
The gate of oneness of cause and effect is thrown open.
The path of nonduality, non-threefoldness right ahead,
Form being the form of no-form,
Going and coming back is right where you are.
Thought is the thought of no-thought.
Singing and dancing are the voice of the Dharma.
How boundless and free is the sky of samadhi.
How refreshingly bright, the moon of the Fourfold Wisdom.
At this moment, what is it you seek? Nirvana is right here before you.
Pure Land is right here.
This body, the body of the Buddha.

—*"Zazen Wasan"* or "Song of Zazen" by Master Hakuin (1685–1768)

Hakuin Ekaku (1685–1758) was a Zen priest who lived during the Tokugawa (pre-modern) period of Japan. He is considered one of the great figures of Japanese Buddhism, and the "second founder" of Rinzai Zen in Japan, as he laid the foundations for a revival of this school at a time when it was in a period of degeneration. During Hakuin's life, the Rinzai school of Zen was caught up in sectarianism and petty rivalries. Amidst this background, Hakuin became a living manifestation of the Zen life, and he thus reinvigorated the entire tradition with his powerful presence and his teaching grounded on his own deep Zen realization.

Early on in his life, Hakuin experienced the harsh realities of existence, and entered a monastery at the age of fifteen. An enlightenment experience can be triggered by different things. It is said that for Shakyamuni it was the twinkle of the morning star that ushered in the experience that revolutionized his universe, and our own. But for Hakuin it was the sound of a temple bell. At twenty-four he came to a deep experience of realization. It is said that he had been sitting all night long, and as he heard the temple bell sounding, he found liberation from all the issues he had been struggling with.

When he was thirty-three years old, Hakuin went back to his home and became caretaker of his father's temple. At that time Japan was divided into jurisdictions of the various Buddhist temples, as part of the plan of the Tokugawa regime to supervise and control the populace. Everyone had to register at a given temple or Shinto shrine in his or her area, rather like the parish system in the Catholic Church during the medieval period of Europe. This was so the Japanese government could monitor the movements of the people, and make sure that there were no Christians in their midst. And so, from the time he was thirty-three until his death at the age of eighty, Hakuin was a simple country temple priest. And yet his career, uneventful from an outward standpoint, embodied the fullness of the awakened life.

Hakuin did not write great tomes, but he had a grasp of the intricacies of Buddhist doctrine and occasionally wrote treatises on various Zen themes. His life, writing, and teaching occasioned a revival of Zen that made its mark throughout the country of Japan in the succeeding centuries. And yet for all this he was a very practical and pastoral person, concerned with the well-being of the people around him, with special concern for the poor and sick. He was also famous for his calligraphy.

The poem that opens this chapter is called "Zazen Wasan." *Wasan* means "praise," and this is a song of praise to Zen, a song of acclamation: "How beautiful! How exquisite!" This song comes from Hakuin's inner state of enlightenment, and in chanting or reciting it, we are invited to go into that inner realm within ourselves. It must be chanted or sung in the context of our very own zazen experience, that is, our own search for our True Self.

The song divides naturally into three parts. I will outline them in brief, and then in detail. The first line up to the line "How can they be freed from the circle of birth and death?" is an introductory section that outlines the entire presupposition of Zen, centered on the opening line, "All sentient beings are originally Buddhas."

The second section begins "As to the Zen of the Great Vehicle" and ends with "how refreshingly bright, the moon of the Fourfold Wisdom." This section is the heart of the text. It explains many Buddhist terms and several other points that require an understanding of Buddhist background. This section gives us the crux of Zen, which as an invitation to experience. This second part describes some of the content of what we are meant to experience.

The third section comprises the last four lines, and is a summary of sorts. The whole song is summed up in the last few words, "This body, the body of the Buddha." In a nutshell we can say that this is our intent—that is, to grasp and taste what those words stand for, "This body, the body of the Buddha."

SONG OF ZAZEN, PART I

"All sentient beings are originally Buddha." This is an expression of the core truth of what we are. It is an exceedingly positive view of our existence, affirming that these finite, ignorant, selfish, and confused beings that we are, are in fact beings endowed with infinite capacity, whose true nature consists in wisdom and compassion.

A comparable statement in the Christian tradition would be the doctrine that we human beings are made in the image of God. "So God created humans in God's own image, in the image of God they were created, male and female God created them"(Genesis 1:27). Based on this fundamental affirmation of our nature as created in the divine image, the Eastern Orthodox tradition in Christianity has continued to uphold the doctrine about the ultimate destiny of human beings as the return to our divine nature, that is, our "divinization" *(theosis)*, through the grace bestowed in Christ, regarded as the firstborn of all creation, the archetype upon whom the rest of us are modeled. One notable difference, however, between the Christian view and the Buddhist view is that in Christianity the "capacity for the divine" is considered as belonging properly to humans only, and not to animals and other species of living beings, whereas in Buddhism all sentient beings, including hell-dwellers, hungry ghosts, malign spirits, and animals, are seen as endowed with the capacity for buddhahood. Thirteenth-century Japanese Zen master Dogen further broadened this notion of "sentient being" to include mountains and rivers, and all the myriad things of the universe.

We are invited to take this affirmation that "all sentient beings are originally Buddhas," and realize it, as applying to each and everyone of us. *Who, me?,* we may ask. *Yes, you,* comes the answer. But we balk at this, not able to accept the tremendous implications of such an affirmation, perhaps with a sense of false humility, perphaps with incredulity and hesitancy at letting go of our view of ourselves as finite, ignorant, selfish, confused beings.

The monk who asked Chao-chou, "Does a dog have Buddha-nature?" was perhaps also plagued by incredulity, not being able to take this exceedingly positive affirmation that applies to all sentient beings. Chao-chou's response was, of course, *"Mu!"*—"No, not by any means!" or "Not in a million years!" But if we take this reading, Chao-chou would be contradicting this fundamental affirmation of his whole tradition of Buddhism. This reading of a negative response to the question would merely bring us back to the obvious fact that a dog is (only) a dog, and I am (only) a finite, ignorant, self-ish, confused human being.

Another koan has Chao-chou responding in the affirmative: "Yes, the dog has Buddha-nature." This version thus is (apparently) a stark contradiction of the other version. This reading of an affirmative response, however, would serve merely our intellectual curiosity about the original nature of the dog. "Yes, of course, our whole Buddhist tradition affirms it. All sentient beings have Buddha-nature. This dog is a sentient being. Therefore, it is elementary, my dear Watson, that, Yes, this dog does have Buddha-nature." If we extend the syllogism to ourselves, we can say, "I too am a sentient being. All sentient beings have Buddha-nature. Therefore, I too have Buddha-nature." Well and good. But such a syllogism does not have the power to bring us anywhere except perhaps to victory in a debating tournament. How does it change the fact that I am (only) a finite, ignorant, selfish, confused human being?

Whether we take no or yes for an answer to the monk's question, we are still left where we started. The clue to unraveling this koan is in taking neither: neither having nor not having, neither being nor non-being. We are invited to take this word, or better, sound, of Mu as a key that will unlock the secrets of our innermost being. This is by repeating this sound of Mu with every outbreath, and repeating it again and again, until the conscious I that is watching this breath, that gets lost in this or that distracting thought, merges with the sound Mu, and becomes one with Mu.

Becoming one with Mu in a state of unitive awareness, or samadhi, is the key to the experiential realization of this opening line of Hakuin's "Song": "All sentient beings are originally Buddhas."

To offer a Christian angle, we can take the affirmation that all things in the universe manifest Divine Presence. Philosophers and theologians of the monotheistic traditions (notably Judaism, Christianity, and Islam) agree on the doctrine of God's omnipresence; there is no place in the universe where God is not. This of course is not equivalent to saying that everything *is* God ("pantheism"), but simply that every single thing in the whole universe exists only insofar as God wills that thing to exist and continues to uphold it in existence. This would embrace not just human beings, but also all beings, including rocks and mountains, stars and galaxies, as well as all forms of vegetable and animal life. This is another way of saying that "everything is in God, and God is in everything." This is a theological position that conforms with orthodox Christianity, sometimes referred to as "pan-entheism." Thus, at least on the doctrinal level, we might find this statement, that "all things in the universe manifest Divine Presence," a closer parallel to the Buddhist affirmation that "all sentient beings are originally Buddhas."

Given this affirmation, a monk could perhaps equivalently ask a Christian mystic, say, Saint John of the Cross, "Does a dog also manifest Divine Presence?" Putatively, Saint John of the Cross would respond, *"Nada."* So we are back to the same place where the Zen monk was, asking Chao-chou about the dog. And the only recourse left to us then would be to sit still in silence, take this *"Nada"* as our guide, and delve deep into the recesses of our being, *"Nada, nada, nada."*

This is an invitation to enter into the Realm of Heaven.

"The Realm of God is at hand. Open your hearts to receive the Good News!" (Mark 1:15). What is the Good News? Just that: The Realm of God is at hand! It is in our very midst!

"All things in the universe manifest Divine Presence." Sitting in silent contemplation is our way of opening our heart to that Presence. This is also what we are invited to when we sit in Zen. We are invited to prepare ourselves for an experience of conversion, of transformation, a *metanoia,* to enable that Realm of God to overpower us, take possession of us, and thus be inundated with this Presence in our entire lives.

All our efforts, however, are but our frail human attempts to prepare ourselves to receive that overpowering reality. What can we do? We straighten our posture, regulate our breathing, and silence our minds. As we do so, we deepen our capacity for concentration. In other words, we attend to the centering of our being.

Ordinarily we find ourselves dispersed in many directions. We rush to make our appointments here and there, we are fragmented in time, and we live in separate compartments. We exert efforts toward various goals that nevertheless do not offer us a sense of fulfillment, of wholeness.

Our zazen can direct us toward a wholeness, as we find ourselves in the direction of centering our being, in focusing on the here and now. The power that arises from sitting comes to be felt, and with it, we come closer to an integration of ourselves, through the practice of taking a relaxed and yet attentive seated posture, regulating our breathing, and silencing the mind, focusing on the here and now.

We are able to be present more and more to our whole being. To become more and more whole…this is the direction we are led to in our sitting in zazen. Its opposite is to be dispersed, separate, every few minutes doing something else, being somewhere else, and thus being the "nowhere man" that the Beatles sang about.

As we deepen our awareness in the silence of seated meditation, we can sense our whole lives as permeated with this wholeness, whereby every moment we are totally and completely in this moment. And this moment is complete and whole, as the previous moment was complete and whole. We are able to experience our lives in completion, in every here and now. It is toward this wholeness that we are moving as we make every step. From this state of awareness, we can glimpse the realm out of which comes the first line of Hakuin's "Song": "All sentient beings are originally Buddhas." Or, "All things in the universe manifest Divine Presence."

Thus, this first section of the Song of Zazen is an acclamation based on the inner state of the Zen life. It is an expression that emanates from living that Zen life. Each one of us is called to enter that world for ourselves, with every breath, with every step. And as we chant or recite this song wholeheartedly and give ourselves to the chanting or recitation, we can get a taste of what that world is all about.

SONG OF ZAZEN, PART II

In Genesis we read that God looked at all of creation, at each and every single creature, and God saw that it was all good! (Genesis 1:1–31) This goodness is the participation of the whole of creation in the Divine Goodness. This fact should not remain in our heads as a concept. We are invited to taste that Goodness. That Goodness we taste is the infinite Goodness that is God.

"All things in the universe manifest Divine Presence." In other words, the earth, the sun, the moon, the plants, birds of the air, are in themselves manifestations of this Presence. Just as they are.

Experiencing "the way things are" is what Zen is. Truly, all we have to "do" is just *be the way we are*. If we grasp this, then the *fact* of Zen will come to us. We will know that the divine Goodness, which permeates all things, is really *this* goodness of standing up, sitting down, laughing, crying. To know something intellectually and to know it experientially are different indeed. We can know intellectually the properties of electricity, but that's nothing like being hit with a live wire!

An experience of the Jewish philosopher Martin Buber comes to mind. As a young boy he loved nature, and one evening after supper, he was in the barn patting the nape of his pet horse, and something happened to him. Later, trying to put it into words, he said that the life force that came from the horse was the same life force that ran through his hands, the same life that runs through the earth, the same life that runs through the whole universe, and that somehow that life infused him at the instant of patting the horse. So, "All things in the universe manifest Divine Presence" became for him not a doctrine but a concrete experience that transformed his whole life.

As a college student, another now famous Catholic theologian was an articulate agnostic. One day, not being able to concentrate on a boring lecture, he glanced out the window and saw new young leaves sprouting from a tree. Suddenly something came through him. He was later to explain that he realized the life coming through those new leaves was the same life that penetrated the tree itself, and was the same life that vivified him as he sat in the classroom. It was the same life that enabled everything to exist. Having experienced this, he could no longer be an atheist. At that instant he could no longer have any doubt about the "existence of God."

Let us not be misled by those words, "the existence of God." The words point to an experiential realization of simple facts. The fact is, that leaves are green; the horse's neck is rough and hairy to the touch; the wind blows; summer is hot, and winter cold. These simple facts enable us to experience what it is, *just as it is,* and thereby to be permeated with this Divine Presence.

The "Song of Zazen" says, "As in the case of water and ice, there is no ice without water." We would not say this if we depended only on our senses. When we feel water we know it is not ice, because ice does not feel like that. Ice is hard, our senses tell us. Our senses tend to delude us and say, "Ice does not feel like water, therefore it is a different thing, separate from and other than water." Our Buddha-nature is like this.

Many times in our daily lives we are deluded by our senses, and we are led to think that things are as our senses would have them be. We need to be "straightened out" in this regard. How?

Perhaps by massage! Many Japanese are very good at massage. A good masseuse can tell you by just touching your shoulder whether you are tense or not, often sensing tension you yourself are not aware of. We tense up because we are not fully at home with ourselves and the way we are. But a mere physical massage can never really "straighten out" what really needs straightening out—our fundamental stance toward our very own nature. So, something equivalent to a spiritual massage may be needed to loosen us up, to enable us to relax, and just *be,* accepting ourselves just as we are, rather than always trying to put up a front to hide our own insecurities and anxieties or to fill in an imagined lack within ourselves. Once we recognize this as our situation, that is, a situation of being ill at ease with ourselves, in short, in a dis-eased condition, we can hear the words of the philosopher Heidegger referring to us when he says, "Let beings be." Let yourself be you as you are, and not something else. The wonder of "you as you are" can never be expressed in words and can only be contemplated in its splendor, with awe and gratitude.

Theologian Paul Tillich makes this very point in an essay of his, "You Are Accepted," published in a collection entitled *Shaking the Foundations.* In short, we need only be humble enough to accept the fact that *we are accepted,* just as we are, no matter what, by that cosmic love that permeates throughout the universe.

This is another significant angle to the Divine Presence alluded to here that our experience of sitting in stillness can bring home to us, namely, that it is a Loving Presence. It is an intimately palpable sense of being affirmed, confirmed, embraced in a cosmic kind of way.

Jesus heard these words as he received baptism from John the Baptist at the river Jordan: "You are my Beloved, in whom I am well pleased" (Mark 1:11). Sitting in stillness, a moment of grace may arrive wherein we are also able to hear these words resound throughout our whole being, and throughout the universe. Trembling, we ask, "Who, me?" And the answer is, "Yes, you!"

> *Not realizing that Truth is so close,*
> *Beings seek it far way—alas!*
> *It is like one who, while being in the midst of water,*

Cries out for thirst.
It is like the child of a rich household
Who gets lost in a poor village.

In another translation, we read, "Not knowing how close the truth is to them, beings seek it afar...what a pity!" Not knowing we are embraced by an infinitely Loving Presence, we are deluded into thinking we are miserable and distorted and separated from our true selves. We feel separated because we are not cognizant of this Presence, which is in fact "more intimate to us than we are to ourselves," as Saint Augustine observed.

What is the root of this separation from our basic goodness, which is the divine Goodness? Is it not our preoccupation with our narrow selves? Is it not our attachments and selfish desires and our pursuit of disparate objects that we think will make us happy, but which only make us more miserable? This is at the root of our misery: We tend to look at things and view them as "objects" separate from us. This way of looking at things divides us at the core of our being.

I'm here, you're there. I am "in here," the world is "out there," and we think that is the way things are. How sad that in our ordinary consciousness we are unable to bridge this gap that separates our little selves from those other beings whose companionship we long for, communion with whom we yearn for from deep in our hearts.

Yet the message resounds. "The Realm of God is at hand. Open your hearts and welcome the Good News." (Mark 1:15) To accept this basic message is what can cut away the Original Sin that separates us from God.

We are made in the image and likeness of God, and our ultimate destiny is to return to God, in realizing who we are, that is, as God's very own image and likeness. We are indeed the rich household's child, though sad to say, we are unaware of our riches. This is our "original sin," that we have forgotten who we truly are.

There is a Mahayana Buddhist parable about the scion of a rich household wanting to leave home and go to all the regions of the world he had never seen before. Before letting him go, the mother sewed a precious jewel in the collar of his son's robe. Everywhere he went, the young man had with him inestimable wealth in that jewel secretly hidden in his collar, but of course he didn't know this.

Eventually, during his travels, he ran out of money. He was hungry and dirty and tired, but unable to do anything about it, or so he thought. He knew nothing of the wealth he was carrying around! Each one of us possesses that richness, if only we knew where to look.

And that is the exhortation of the "Song of Zazen," "Look, you have wealth with you. Open your eyes to discover it, put it to good use. Unpack it. Live it!"

> *The reason why beings transmigrate through the six realms*
> *Is because they are lost in the darkness of ignorance.*
> *Wandering about from darkness to darkness*
> *How can they be freed from the cycle of birth and death?*

Indian tradition speaks of six realms of living beings who keep on being reborn and dying without ever reaching eternal happiness, a dreary existence always in the midst of suffering. Ignorance is the cause of suffering, which prevents us from seeing what we truly are.

We wander from "dark path to dark path." Our daily lives are filled with such things as greed and anger, discouragement, depression. Everyone is out for himself or herself. We all stand in conflict with one another. In our human society it is a truism to say that the powerful exploit the weak. Those who are exploited go on to exploit others, and the vicious circle continues. This is part of what is meant by transmigration, as we go around in circles, unable to realize true happiness as we look at and relate with one another from our narrow egoistic perspectives.

How are we to be freed from this cycle of unhappiness? We can be freed by the realization of who or what we are, or in other words, by awakening to the reality of ourselves, our True Selves. How do we awaken to this True Self? This happens when we see with our inner eyes that we are indeed embraced in a Loving Presence that affirms us, accepts us just as we are, just as everyone else, everything else, is accepted as they are.

As we say in Zen, to see into one's nature is by that very fact to *become* Buddha. Here, to "become" does not mean to turn into something that one was not, but rather, to reclaim what one has been right from the start. To see and to accept that we are born in the divine image, and breathe every breath, take every step throughout our lives in the midst of a Loving Presence, is to realize our true freedom as children of God.

> *As to the Zen samadhi of the Great Vehicle*
> *No amount of praise can exhaust its treasures.*
> *The six Ways to perfection, beginning with Giving,*
> *Living a right life, and other good deeds,*
> *Intoning the name of Buddha, Repentance, and so on,*
> *All these come down to the merit of Zen sitting.*

This is exclamation of the highest praise, extolling the many virtues that arise from Zen *samadhi*—a Sanskrit term that can be rendered simply as "deep meditation." To be in deep meditation is to be unmoving amid or to be unmoved by everything. Samadhi is unmoved, and yet it is the power that moves everything. It is the dynamic Mover of everything that does not itself move.

"O, the Zen samadhi of the Great Vehicle." In samadhi we enter the very source of movement of the universe itself, as we reach that "still point of the turning world," to borrow from a poem by T. S. Eliot. In our Zen practice we enter into that dynamic center of the universe that is complete, perfect, fully calm, yet full of energy. In this calm originates the power that moves the whole universe. It is that into which we plunge ourselves as we sit in Zen.

This is the inner disposition we are called upon to arrive at in our daily lives. We can be perfectly calm, and yet fully dynamic. We are not agitated in our dealings with others. We neither push ourselves nor do we push others. We are to be what we are, and accept one another as we are. In so doing, the power that lies latent will naturally activate itself, and it is the power that can transform the world.

This is the object of praise. It is a state that encompasses all the other devotional and ascetical practices. All are contained in Zen sitting. In other words, what we realize in entering into samadhi is something that contains all the virtues extolled in Buddhist tradition, including the perfections of giving, right conduct, and all the others. Robert Aitken's wonderful book *The Practice of Perfection* is a superb exploration of the these great virtues.

SONG OF ZAZEN, PART III

"Behold, I come to make all things new" (Revelations 21:5). The newness of every moment is what we are called by the "Song" to taste
and experience. That is why the next line says, "The merit of even a
single sitting in Zen erases the countless sins of the past," or as
another translation has it, "One sitting sweeps away all ancient vices."
In the eternal moment there is no past or future. We are living in the
eternal present, before the foundation of the world and yet also at the
culmination of time, when all things in heaven and earth are gathered
as one. We are called to taste and grasp that *now* at every moment of
our lives. If we think of this with our discursive mind, caught in the
framework of linear time and geometric space, we will be bogged
down by conceptual contradictions. So we are called to set aside this
discursive mind and to see with the eyes of our heart the world of the
eternal now that opens us to the realm of the infinite.

> *Where then are the evil ways that can mislead us?*
> *The Pure Land cannot be far away.*

In the New Testament, when Jesus went to the synagogue and
read a passage from the text of Isaiah, he proclaimed to his hear-
ers, "Behold, these words of scripture are fulfilled *now* before your
very eyes" (Luke 4:21). And Hakuin tells us, "The Pure Land cannot be far away." The Realm of Heaven is at hand. Let us cup our
ears to hear it. Let us open our inner eyes to see it.

> *Those who even once, with a humble disposition*
> *Are able to hear this Truth*
> *Praise it and faithfully adhere to it*
> *Will be endowed with innumerable merits.*

Or as another translation puts it, "The one who hears the script but
once, listens to it with a grateful heart, exalting it and revering it,
gains blessings without end." Just one experience of genuine hearing
is enough! There is a famous koan: "What is the sound of one hand
clapping?" One true hearing of this sound is all we need. The single
experience of Shakyamuni under the bodhi tree revolutionized his

entire life. For many of us, it is the one true moment when we can really hear the primal Word and are enabled to see our True Selves. This moment will be forever, and we will be changed forever because of that one experience.

There is a Chinese proverb every Japanese child memorizes when he or she studies Confucian thought. An approximate translation is, "When one is able to hear the Way in the morning, one can die in peace in the evening." If one is really able to see the Way, the Truth, and the Life, even in one glimpse, then that's sufficient. One is ready to die in contentment.

These are akin to the words of my teacher Yamada Roshi immediately following his experience of *satori*. It was so profound that it revolutionized his entire universe, and he was able to say, "I am ready to die. Even if I die at this moment, my life would have infinite value because of this one experience."

Those of us who have experienced even a small glimpse of this Realm may be able to say the same. That glimpse at that moment is enough to make us realize that our life is of infinite worth. Even if we die at that very moment, we have no fear of pain or death. We are ready for anything, because we have already received an infinity of richness. We realize that there is nothing at all to lose. The Truth we experience in this way is obviously not a kind of exalted universal principle that one comes to understand after laborious reasoning and discursive thinking. It can be triggered by some little sensation—the ticking of a clock, the clapping of hands, the breaking of a bucket—simple facts of daily existence, under our very noses!

Our lives will end in tragedy if we go astray, looking for the Truth afar, not realizing that it is right here! How unfortunate that we find it hard to see and hear the things that are so close to us.

Let us listen to these simple facts of our daily living. Our lives come to fruition not in some glorious, idealized future, but with every fact and event right here in the midst of our day-to-day existence.

This is the central message of Christianity, namely, the very reality of "God with us." The Word become flesh. God become human. When we grasp what it means to be human, truly human, we may be able to glimpse that all-embracing, Divine, Loving Presence.

But if you turn your gaze within
And attest to the Truth of essential-nature
That self-nature that is no-nature
You will have gone beyond mere sophistry.

It is not easy to "turn your gaze within" because in the Awakened Realm, there is no within or without. On the practical level this is telling us that we are distracted by things outside ourselves, because we (as subjects) pursue them as objects, which automatically puts them "outside" ourselves. We listen to sounds "out there." We see things "out there." We relate to people "over there." The "Song" tells us to stop looking out and to look within. We do this by cutting out the distinction of outside and inside. Everything is seen from within, because we are all in the same world, inside the Realm, permeated by a Divine, Loving Presence.

This, of course, does not mean that we look at our psychological impressions and reactions because that, too, is taking those impressions and reactions as objects, and putting us "outside" again! If this is a way of seeing that cuts through the subject-object distinction, how can the eye see itself? We will come to that in the next stanza of the "Song."

"Attesting to the truth" means simply realizing clearly. And in realizing our self-nature we find that in its actualization, it is no-nature. Now we have a contradiction. How is that? We may return here to the image of the fraction that Yamada Roshi uses, with zero-infinity as the denominator. There is nothing there! We are nothing before the infinity of that Divine, Loving Presence. Turning inward, we are called to return to that nothingness out of which we were created, and there we will see the face of God.

The face of God is the Original Face in whose image we were created. That's what we are asked to present in the koan, "Show me your original face before your parents were born." That face cannot be seen unless we return to the nothingness of our nature, "before the foundation of the world, holy and blameless…destined in love" (Ephesians 1:3–4). In the dokusan room, at a private meeting with the Zen teacher, we may be asked outright: "Show me that face." This question cannot be answered through mere cleverness, because analytically it is nonsense. There is no use trying to figure it out with the rational, discursive mind. For this is an invitation to an experience of that ineffable Divine, Loving Presence.

> *The gate of oneness of cause and effect is thrown open.*
> *The path of the nonduality, non-threefoldness right ahead…*

The relationship of cause and effect is something that is always mentioned in Buddhist philosophy—whenever we are sidetracked into intellectualizing. The second koan in the *Gateless Gate* talks about whether the enlightened person is free from cause and effect. The gist of this can be gleaned from this stanza of the "Song": Cause and effect are one; not two, not three; the path runs straight.

There is another koan that asks us to "Walk straight on a narrow mountain road that has ninety-nine curves." Being confronted with a conceptual contradiction has its purpose in Zen practice: it frustrates the rational mind that wants to solve things by syllogism and logic, and allows original Mind to see things as they are come forth, straight on, no curves.

> *Form being the form of no-form*
> *Going and coming back is right where you are.*
> *Thought is the thought of no-thought.*
> *Singing and dancing are the voice of Truth.*

The "form and no-form, thought and no-thought" go together, from a Chinese phrase pronounced in Japanese *munen-muso,* "no thought, no image." Actually, this is a bit misleading in words, because how can you have no thought, no form when you are sitting and saying, "I have no thought"? That's already one thought! To say we have no thought or no form boggles the mind and pushes us into a corner. We can't cut the vicious circle.

How can we realize this no-form and no-thought? Simply by settling down and letting ourselves *be.* When we're hot, we just wipe off the sweat without reflecting on the heat. When we're thirsty and take a drink we are just one with the moment, being ourselves with the moment, fully, totally. Not to think, but to *be,* is the secret.

Another translation of the second phrase says, "Your going and coming, never astray." This tells us there is no coming or going, and yet, even in always moving to and fro, one is always still. Nonsense again! We see our world moving in the phrase of Heraclitus, "Everything moves, everything flows." And yet another Greek thinker, Parmenides, says, "Nothing moves, everything is one." What we are seeking is a reconciliation of those two: Everything moves, yet everything is still. We are where we are. We keep on moving dynamically and yet nothing has to move, everything complete and at peace as it is. In the Realm of Heaven "death will be no more, mourning and crying and pain will be no more" (Revelations 21:4).

The last phrase in the stanza is "Singing and dancing are the voice of Truth." Singing and dancing are a full expression of the truth of the Dharma. "So, whether you eat or drink, or whatever you do, do all to the glory of God" (1 Corinthians 10:31). When we dance, and really *dance,* we are in a state of *"munen-muso,"* no-form, no-thought, but *just dancing.*

I remember a celebration after a *sesshin* we held under the guidance of Yamada Roshi in Leyte, Philippines, in the early 1980s, as an act of commemoration and reparation for those who died in the Second World War. Leyte was the place of a ferocious battle between the Japanese forces on the one hand, and the allied Filipino and American forces on the other, that resulted in many casualties on both sides.

After the retreat, we had a reception and party in the same hall where we had sat in zazen, and many were led in the exuberance of the moment to dance to the background music. Yamada Roshi was watching us intently, enjoying what he was seeing. As the music quieted down a bit, he commented out loud to the crowd— "How can you not get enlightened? You all dance so well!"

> *How boundless and free is the sky of samadhi,*
> *How refreshingly bright, the moon of the Fourfold Wisdom!*

We come to samadhi, the inner world of stillness, which manifests itself dynamically in the movement of the universe: "The clear blue sky with no trace of cloud to mar the gazing eye." Our eyes confront things before us that are the cause of our delusions, insofar as we regard them as "objects out there." As we are able to break through this thought of "objects out there," and see things "just as they are," everything becomes like a clear blue sky. The moon shines brightly. We don't even need a finger to point to the moon. All we have to do is let it shine in all its splendid brilliance. Just as it is.

At this moment, what is it you seek?
Nirvana is right here before you
Pure Land is right here.
This body, the body of the Buddha.

These last four lines are a summary of Hakuin's entire "Song." A more familiar translation is, "And what more indeed can we seek; here is nirvana itself revealed; this very place is the Lotus Land; this very body, the Buddha."

Everything is here, complete and total. What more indeed can we seek? We are nothing, created out of nothing, and yet complete, perfect just as we are, in our very nothingness. The glimpse of that nothingness is precisely the key to our completion, perfection, peace and freedom. The "Song" invites us to this experience of nothingness in completion, perfection in nothingness.

"Here is nirvana itself revealed." Not way up in the heavens, but right here under our noses. This basic message has been sadly overlooked, and that is why Marx criticizes religion as being a pie in the sky. People look up to the sky, or to the next life, or to some idealized future, for the fulfillment of their desires, for the realization of happiness. This attitude makes us forget and neglect the treasure that lies in the here and now. We are invited to open our eyes, and open our hearts. Lo and behold, the Realm of Heaven is at hand.

"This very place is the Lotus Land." Let us not misunderstand this phrase to mean that we are already in heaven. Goodness, there is still a whole world to be transformed! The whole of creation is groaning in pain, toward its fulfillment (Romans 8:19). And with each groan, the "already here" and the "not yet" come together. The Realm is realized and yet is still to be fulfilled. This contradiction becomes resolved upon entering the Realm. The here and now is complete and perfect, and yet it calls for a greater perfection and greater wholeness. That

Divine, Loving Presence that we call God, is always beyond, transcending everything we can ever imagine, and yet more intimate to us than we are to ourselves.

The last phrase says "This very body, the body of Buddha." This body of ours right here is not our accustomed image of the Buddha, the one so serenely depicted on altars and sacred paintings.

To see this from another angle, let us consider what happens at the Christian Eucharistic celebration, the Mass. The central event of this ritual consists in the words of consecration, uttered by the priest, in remembrance of what Jesus Christ said during his last supper with his disciples, just before he was put to death on the Cross. He takes the bread, and says, "This is my body, given for you."

If we listen with our hearts here, what do we have? "This is my body." What is "this"? Who is "my"? And what is this "body"? And who is this "you"? As we are able to hear, from the core of our being, these words of consecration, "This is my body, given for you," the barrier between this narrow self with this given physical body, and all the bodies of all sentient beings, and the bodies of all the saints, and this whole earth, and the whole universe, and the body of Christ, collapses. And with this collapse, we see with new eyes, and we hear with new ears, the sound out of the depths: "This is my body, given for you."

If we live only at the surface level of our consciousness, we are but puny little separate beings, and I am here and Jack is over there, and Jill is on the other side. We are different and dispersed. But if we are able to go to a deeper level, we see the point where there is no separation whatsoever. We are "this body." As we experience this Realm of "this body," we are able to experience the ground of com-passion, literally, suffering-with. The suffering of our fellow living beings has become our very own, no longer something apart from us. "This is my body, given for you."

"This very body" is the body of each and every one of us groaning in pain and struggling in suffering in this world of ours. As we are able to utter from the depths of our being these words, "This is my body, given for you," we realize, with eyes now wide open, this very body, the body of Buddha.

The
Enlightened
Samaritan
A ZEN READING OF A CHRISTIAN PARABLE

THE FOLLOWING PIECE IS presented with the initial disclaimer that my intention is not to make a "commentary" on a scriptural passage. I say this because the scripture points to a *living reality* that we are invited to enter into and not just observe from the outside and comment upon. Another way of putting it is that we are presented with spiritual *food*. And, just as with any food, the appropriate response is not just to gaze upon it or take pictures of it—although it is perfectly legitimate to do so—but to *partake of and eat* what is before us. So it is with this attitude that we are invited to enter into the world of this scripture passage. We read not only with our heads but also with our body, with our whole being, entering into the living world of the text and allowing that dynamic life to envelop us, with every breath, with every pulse.

Consider this parable from the Gospels:

On one occasion a lawyer came forward to put this test question to him: "Master, what must I do to inherit eternal life?" Jesus said, "What is written in the law? What is your reading of it?" He replied, "Love the Lord your God with all your heart, with all your soul, with all your strength, and with all your mind; and your neighbor as yourself." "That is the right answer," said Jesus; "do that and you will live."

But he wanted to vindicate himself, so he said to Jesus, "And who is my neighbor?" Jesus replied, "A man was on his way from Jerusalem down to Jericho when he fell in with robbers, who stripped him, beat him, and went off, leaving him half dead. It so happened that a priest was going down by the road; but when he saw him, he went past on the other side. So too, a Levite came to the place, and when he saw him went past to the other side. But a Samaritan who was making the journey came upon him and when he saw him was moved to pity. He went up and bandaged his wounds, bathing them with oil and wine. Then he lifted him on to his own beast, brought him to an inn, and looked after him there. Next day, he produced two silver pieces and gave them to the innkeeper, and said 'Look after him; and if you spend any more, I will repay you on my way back.' Which of these three do you think was neighbor to the man who fell into the hands of the robbers?" He answered, "The one who showed him kindness." Jesus said, "Go and do as he did" (Luke 10:25–37).

We tend to read this passage as moral injunction: "Help your neighbor in need." While that may be one valid reading it would not do full justice to what is being presented to us here.

It begins with the question of the lawyer, "What must I do to attain eternal life?" Let us plumb the depths of our being and really hear this question. This is the very question we ourselves are asking in our hearts, although we may put it in different ways:

What is true living?
How may I live an authentic life?
How may I realize who I am, and live my True Self
each moment of my life?

"Eternal life" thus is not life after we die, the extension of some form of consciousness that will go on after our biological death, but something that is available here and now.

It points to the same reality that is indicated in another New Testament passage, "The Realm of God is at hand!" (Mark 1:15)— right here! How are we to partake of eternal life in the here and now before us?

The passage is not about somehow "meriting entry into this eternal life "because" we have done good for our neighbor—although this is a common interpretation of longstanding. That indeed is a very narrow reading, which I assert distorts the text. We are invited to pause in silence in asking this question, "What *is* eternal life?

What we are looking for in reading this passage of New Testament scripture is not so much the "meaning" of the text but an inroad into the search in which we are engaged, the search for the answer to the questions, "Who am I?" and "What is my True Self?"

Now, with that disposition, we are prepared to enter the world of the text, not just mentally, but also bodily, with our entire being.

Our quest is itself the search for eternal life. That is what we are earnestly seeking as we sit in silence, paying attention to our breathing, focusing our entire being in the here and now. For those who are practicing with the koan Mu, this is likewise at the bottom of the whole enterprise. In the practice of this koan, we breathe in and out with Mu, sit with Mu, stand with Mu, walk with Mu, until we come to a point wherein we are dissolved into Mu. And when that happens, it is no longer *I* that breathes, that sits, that stands, that walks. Only Mu. When Mu manifests itself, we realize that we have entered the realm of eternal life.

In the parable above, we are told that the key to eternal life is acquired by following this hallowed commandment: "Love the Lord God with all your heart, with all your soul, and with all your strength, and with all your mind." For those of us who have been raised in the Christian tradition, these words are so familiar to us that they tend to go all but unheard—in one ear and out the other. But this time, let us ask ourselves, what does this commandment really ask of us? Does this loving of God with our whole mind involve some special kind of activity, some special way of thinking or feeling?

Or perhaps we can ask the same question in a different way, looking at the tasks already before us that we repeat day in and day out: How do we love God with our whole mind and whole heart and whole being while, say, driving a car? Or, how do we love God when washing dishes (or loading the dishwasher), while waiting in line at the post office, or pushing the grocery cart back to the car? How do we love God with our whole being when we are sleeping? How do we love God in that way when told we have cancer, or when we are in terrible pain from illness or injury?

The hint here is that "loving God with our whole heart, our whole mind, our whole strength, our whole being," is not an "additional thing" we do over and above all the little things we do from day to day. What is our day made up of? We get up, wash our face, eat breakfast, go to work, meet people, and so on. As we do all those things with our whole soul, our whole strength, our whole mind, the question stands: How do we love God? In short, the "God" referred to when we say "loving God" is not something "up there" or even "in here" that is the object of our "love." What then is meant by this phrase "loving God"? Another question that may shed light on this one is this: What is "living Zen," in the context of the various events and encounters of our daily life, such as washing our face, eating breakfast, meeting people, and so on?

Pushing the question further, what is this eternal life all about, and where is it to be discovered as we live through all these particular events of our daily life? Perhaps what prevents us from "seeing" what all this is revealing to us is that we go about all these things *not* with our whole whole soul or whole strength or whole mind. We go about our lives in a half-daze, not sure where we are heading, torn in different directions and constantly nagged by an inner voice, saying, "Is *this* all there is?"

Those of us who are able to listen to this voice and take it to heart are those who hear the call to give ourselves a little more leeway in life, to be silent, to look within, perhaps to venture into zazen. In that context, we may come to be disposed, little by little, to clearing away the clutter in our lives, and enabled to listen at and hear from the center of our being. And this can open us up to awakening.

Now let us look at the second clause of the commandment. "And, love your neighbor as yourself." This is a most natural outflow of the first clause, to love God with our whole heart and whole being. In loving God with our whole being, we are able to experience "loving ourselves" in an entirely different way. "Being in love" in this way, with every breath, every step, every act, every encounter in our daily lives, the question may arise: Who is loving? And who is being loved? The question may open us to a new horizon of our lives. That is, we may catch a glimpse of a reality that we can only express by saying: Love is Loving Itself(!). What does this mean? This now sounds like a redundant statement, much like "living Zen" is redundant, or tautologous. For seen in a certain way, "living" is no other than Zen itself, and conversely, "Zen" is no other than living itself.

From this perspective just described, our "neighbor" is also seen in a totally different light. It is no longer "that *other* person that I must be kind to," or some designation of the sort, but one who is included in that circle of Love loving itself. As we see our neigh-bor as not separate from ourselves, but as embraced in the same circle of Love that we ourselves are embraced in, in the same way, we embrace them with our whole soul, our whole mind, our whole heart, our whole strength. This brings to the surface another redundancy, because from the perspective described above, that is, of love loving itself, then, "loving God," "loving ourselves," and "loving our neighbor," are expressions that point to the very same dynamic Reality wherein each of us is enveloped from moment to moment, with every pulse and every breath of our lives!

But then again, we feel the need to ask, who *is* our neighbor, as the lawyer in the passage asks on our behalf. And in response Jesus tells the story of the wounded traveler, the priest, the Levite, and the Samaritan.

Again, if we take this story merely as a moral injunction to help those in need, we easily miss the import of the passage. Such a moralistic reading catches us in a dualistic mentality: separating "I the helper" from "those others in need."

But this is not quite what the passage is about at its deepest level. Here we meet with the word translated into English as *compassion*. This word in Greek (the language in which the New Testament is written) is *splanchnizomai,* and means, literally, "to be moved in one's gut" (closer to the point, "in one's bowels" or "in one's innards"). That is, "being moved to the very depths of one's being." The Latin root of the English word *compassion* means "to suffer with," which, in the Greek, is rendered in a rather "gutsy," bodily kind of way—"to feel the pain of another in one's own gut." In short, the pain of the person lying there on the road is experienced as my very own pain, right at the core of my own being. It is no longer a case of being up on one's donkey saying, "Ah, too bad! That poor fellow! Let me come down and help," as it were from an outsider's standpoint. The Samaritan was "moved, and felt the pain in his very gut." At that very instant he saw through and overcame the barrier of self and other, and the pain of the wounded traveler became manifest as his very own. Jumping off the donkey, treating the wounds, making provisions for shelter and care were but the most natural kind of action to follow. Just as if an itchy feeling arose in my right arm, arm without even thinking, my left hand would move in its direction, my fingers would start scratching, and when they had done their job by relieving the itch, my left hand would go on back doing whatever it was doing before. And all this, without the right hand even "knowing" what the left hand did.

There is a koan in the collection called the *Blue Cliff Record,* which goes like this: Yun-men asked Tao-wu: "What does the Bodhisattva of Compassion make of all those hands and eyes?" Tao-wu said: "It is like adjusting a pillow with an outstretched hand in the middle of the night."

We will look at this Bodhisattva of Compassion with a thousand hands in a later chapter, but here our focus is on the answer: an outstretched hand adjusting a pillow in the middle of the night. It is the middle of the night, the night of emptiness, the night of unknowing. One is asleep. In short, there is no trace of self-consciousness as to what is going on. And in the middle of this, somehow, as my pillow slips off, and my head feels displaced, spontaneously, my hand reaches out to adjust the pillow, and I go back to sleep. That's all. This koan is saying, "*That's* compassion."

It is significant for us to note that what the Samaritan did was not some kind of "supererogatory" good deed, some type of volunteer action, action above and beyond the normal call of duty. Nor in his mind did he perform an "act of charity" for "another," a meritorious act that would help him get a heavenly reward. He merely did immediately the most natural thing to do in that situation. This "most natural thing" is what we do spontaneously when we transcend duality, when we see "the other" as not separate from our own self.

Entering this world of nonduality is what can happen through sitting silently in zazen. And a very effective key to entering this world, paradoxically enough, is—pain! The pain of the world, the pain of my neighbor, even the pain in my knees invites me to plunge into this world of nonduality in an immediate kind of way.

What we "need to do" to enter eternal life is presented to us in this story. But it is not translated into the prescription to "help our neighbor in need," though we are certainly not saying that one should not do so. All the Samaritan "did" was simply the most natural and spontaneous action that would follow upon breaking through the dualistic perception of "I" and "other." It was the pain of the wounded traveler that, to use a Zen term here, became the "turning word" for the Samaritan, opening his heart and mind to enlightened action, activating the power of compassion.

As we look around us, the world is filled with all kinds of possible "turning words" that can open our eyes to this world of nonduality. The trees, the mountains, the sky, stones, rivers, are all saying, "Look at me, and see!" Can you hear them? For some of us whose hearts have been hardened by our own self-preoccupations, or by idealistic expectations that keep us dissatisfied with what is available, or else for those of us who have come to take these wonders for granted, we need to be thrown off our donkey, as it were, by something a little more jolting, like the very real and concrete pain of the trees of the Amazon being felled, the mountains being leveled by mining companies to get the minerals underneath, the earth being polluted by industrial waste. The pain of the refugees in war-torn countries, the pain of the starving children. The pain of those harassed or treated with discrimination due to ethnic origin or skin color or gender or sexual orientation. Or the pain of a friend who has lost a loved one in death. In the last part of the story, Jesus asked, "And who do you think was neighbor to that man in pain?" The lawyer's answer was, "The one who had mercy." Jesus responded, "Go and do as he did."

We should not take this to mean "Go and imitate the Samaritan; do what the Samaritan did." Let us take these words of Jesus as a koan for us to enter into with our whole body and mind. And if we let such a koan do in us what koans usually do in a practitioner, we may just find ourselves thrown off the donkeys of our self-contained securities and plunged into a world of nonduality, a world seeped in Compassion of a cosmic kind. The word "do" may be misleading, so we can perhaps rephrase the response, and say, "Go, and *be* as he *is*." In short, enter into that world of nonduality and Compassion wherein the Samaritan constantly dwells. The direct way to this is by listening to the world's pain. But there is no such thing as "the world's pain" in the abstract. Let us begin by listening to the pain of the person next to us. That may become the turning word that could open our eyes to eternal life.

In Catholic tradition, Mary, the Mother of Jesus, our Blessed Mother, is the epitome of the enlightened person who embodies the wisdom of nonduality. Her song in response to the invitation of the Angel Gabriel to her, that she bear God in her own body, is a chant known in Christian tradition as the Magnificat. This song manifests the clarity of her mind and the purity of her heart. "My soul magnifies the Lord. And my spirit rejoices in God my Savior. For God hath looked with favor upon this servant in her nothingness" (Luke 1:48). In the total emptying of herself, the grace of God enveloped her in a way that overcame all duality. Her every action and indeed her whole life thus came to be a manifestation of the grace of God. That grace of God expressed its fullness in her life when it reached its culmination in her bearing in her own body the suffering of Jesus on the cross. In embracing her own son's suffering, she accepted his suffering for all men and women throughout the ages, in her own body. In Mary we find a veritable embodiment of the world of nonduality and *"com-passion."*

The Samaritan in the passage likewise lived in this world of nonduality. Let us recall the social context presented by scripture scholars who note that the Samaritans were looked down upon by the Jewish people at the time. The Samaritans were considered second-class citizens in that society and were in a situation of oppression and discrimination. The Samaritan, therefore, knew intimately in his own body what pain was. Further, he knew what it was to be despised and discriminated against and to be considered "unclean." The Samaritan in our story, in other words, was very much attuned to living the pain of the world. And so when he saw someone lying on the road in pain, he was already disposed to casting aside the barrier that made him see the wounded traveler as "other" much less as a member of that social class that was oppressing his own people. An immediate experience of oneness with that person in pain came to him naturally and spontaneously, without any "effort" at all. The practice of zazen can help us grow into our own naturalness. Through sitting, we become more readily able to bodily experience the world of nonduality.

The Jewish philosopher Martin Buber's experience of nonduality was in the context of considering a tree, as he describes in his book *I and Thou.* There are many ways we can look at a tree, Buber tells us. We can analyze it, or note its artistry or color and so on. But he continues, there's another way. It is a way of *listening in silence,* whereby we encounter the tree as simply *Here.* That is all. No longer "I" looking at the tree, but just the tree! That's it. No subject, no object, just *Tree.*

It brings to mind a koan in the *Gateless Gate* (case 37). Chao-chou, the same one of the famous *mu*-koan, is asked earnestly by a monk, "Why did the Bodhidharma come from the West?" This is another way of asking, "What is the very heart of the matter in Zen?" or, "What is enlightenment?" We could also phrase it as "What is nonduality?" Chao-chou's answer is simply, "The oak tree in the garden."

Of course there is nothing special about the tree in Chao-chou's answer. It could just as easily be a bird, the tick-tock of the clock, the gurgling of a boiling pot. In the case of the Samaritan, it was the pain of the wounded traveler lying on the road.

Or, to return to the topic raised earlier, we can interpret the question as, "How can we realize eternal life?" The passage we have been considering offers us the hint: Open your heart to the pain of the world. Listen to the pain of your neighbor. This is where we may find our True Self, and this is how we can experience eternal life.

The Four Vows
of the Bodhisattva

THE BODHISATTVA, OR SEEKER-AFTER-WISDOM, is none other than each of us, in earnest search for our True Self, our "original face." As we embark on this search, we make a great resolve comprising four items, which we call the "Four Great Vows." We do this at the commencement of our path to practice, and keep renewing it all through the way. In a similar way, Christians who pursue a religious calling and who formally enter a religious congregation take certain vows, namely vows of poverty, chastity, and obedience to their religious superiors. In professing these vows they publicly express their intention to live no longer according to their own individual whims or desires, but entirely according to God's will, in the service of God's people.

Those who embark on the way of the Bodhisattva, in search of the True Wisdom that flows in Compassion, are called to profess the following four vows:

Sentient beings are numberless; I vow to free them.
Delusions are inexhaustible; I vow to extinguish them all.
The Gates of the Truth are countless; I vow to open them.
The enlightened Way is unsurpassable; I vow to embody it.

Expressing this great resolve, the seekers after wisdom profess that they pursue enlightenment not only for their own narrow satisfaction or individual salvation, but that they seek wisdom for, on behalf of, and together with all living beings. The Bodhisattva therefore is one who seeks the total liberation of all living beings—a great resolve indeed, more like "the impossible dream"!

Some of us may ask ourselves, *How can I presume to free others unless I myself am freed first? How can I enlighten others unless I am first enlightened myself?* And these are apt questions.

However, this mode of questioning is marked by a misleading assumption concerning our relation to others, to all living beings—the assumption of separation. And this assumption can only be genuinely and effectively overcome in the experience of enlightenment itself, whereby I fully realize that I am in all living beings and all living beings are in me. The experience of enlightenment breaks the barrier between myself and others. One who is still at a stage prior to this experience can only take it on faith for the moment, namely, that all living beings are one, partaking of one life, one reality.

In a similar vein, from a Christian angle, one seeking to follow the will of God, may embark on the journey not knowing fully the implications of what one is getting into. Earnest in pursing that call, such a person can only live in faith and trust, that somehow "God is leading me every step along the way." This act of faith is bound to be rewarded by the actual vision of what it promises, when that moment comes. Part of the reward is in the realization that God is with us, loving us, every step along the way, not just "out there," but as Saint Augustine noted, "more intimate to me than I am to myself." The discovery of this loving God as present in the depths of my own being is what breaks down the barrier between myself and others: For I also come to realize that this Loving God loving me is also there loving my neighbor just as I am loved.

Let us now take the four vows of the seeker after wisdom in their particular intent and content.

SENTIENT BEINGS ARE NUMBERLESS;
I VOW TO FREE THEM

This vow calls to mind not just all beings alive now, but the infinite number of living beings that have existed since the beginning of time, as well as those who will exist until the end of time (regardless of how we understand "end" or "beginning" of time).

"Sentient beings" in Buddhist terminology refers to beings trapped in this world of suffering, that is, suffering beings. With this implied sense we are called to perceive the actual situation of the world today, with all its disorder and conflict and suffering.

We are called to witness the situation of nearly 1 billion people who are on the brink of starvation and those deprived of even the basic food, clothing, and shelter necessary for normal human life. Many struggle to survive under unjust conditions and inhuman treatment under oppressive structures, while trying to assert their dignity as human beings in the face of so many structural and manmade obstacles. We are invited to open our eyes to countless people involved or dragged into racial, interethnic, intrapartisan, internecine conflicts and violent struggles, and the numberless individuals and families driven from their homes and homelands by repressive and unbearable conditions, left to fend for themselves as refugees in the industrialized societies of the West, where many people are hostile or at best indifferent to them and treat them as "burdens on the economy." We are invited to look at those numberless people who suffer discriminatory treatment because of race, creed, origin, gender or sexual orientation, or disability.

This list does not even address all those psychological and spiritual sufferings of every sort, from separation of loved ones, to all the modes of existential anguish that can drive even so-called privileged individuals to despair and misery.

The central characteristic of a sentient being, indeed, is this capacity to suffer. Not only the *capacity,* but the actuality of *being in suffering.* So what exactly does the seeker-after-wisdom vow, when he or she vows to free all sentient beings from their suffering? Does the seeker mean to eradicate suffering itself becoming a Mr. or Ms. Fix-it will solve all the problems of the world? What a presumptuous attitude that would be—as if one could be a universal savior!

The hint of an answer to this is found in one of the many "miscellaneous" koans given after the initial breakthrough to Mu, by which the teacher seeks to confirm and clarify the student's breakthrough to the world of nonduality. "Save a wandering spirit," says one koan. The point of the koan is to overcome the opposition between myself and the wandering spirit, in other words, to be one with that wandering spirit in its search for salvation. Those who have passed the koan may have caught the point that the way to save the wandering spirit is the very same as the way to save all sentient beings in suffering. Let me whisper a clue to this koan: In order to save it, *one must become fully at one with the wandering spirit.* This experience of becoming one is the very moment of salvation one is seeking. But the koan goes further still, and this is where my hint must stop. How is that spirit saved? If one has glimpsed that world of nonduality in an experiential way, the answer to this question should be forthcoming from inside oneself. But here all possible conceptual answers are blocked. For by definition, it is the very nature of a wandering spirit to be in dire need of salvation! So one gets caught in a conceptual contradiction that can only be broken with the entry into that Realm that is not-two—and not…and not-one either!

A variation of this koan could be, "Save a child dying of hunger!" If one has experienced the "saving" of the wandering spirit, one also realizes that the "salvation" of the child dying of hunger does not consist merely in a doling out of food. It is something that cuts through us right at the heart of our being, inviting us to plunge into the realities of hunger and malnutrition and starvation in this world of ours.

The late spiritual writer Henri Nouwen calls our attention to the figure of the wounded healer, in a well-known book of that title. This is a concept that comes across with the very same point that this koan invites us to experience.

In order to appreciate what this vow means, the seekers after wisdom are called, first, to break the barrier between themselves and the dying child, between themselves and all living beings. With this understanding, one is opened to an entirely new perspective in looking at this world of suffering, and how to save beings in the midst of it.

DELUSIONS ARE INEXHAUSTIBLE; I VOW TO END THEM

Delusive passions and attachments are a consequence of our blind ignorance, rooted in clinging to a delusive ego. This is the root cause of all the actual suffering of human beings. The delusive ego, operating on the individual level, as well as on social, structural, and all the levels of our interconnected web of being, is the direct cause of the starvation of millions on our planet today, the root cause of unjust and inhuman structures, of the violent struggles between groups and factions that cause a war situation in many places, and the ongoing destruction of the environment that threatens the very survival of our planet. All these and in fact all the suffering and anguish of all human beings can be traced ultimately to the blind and destructive workings of, and our attachment to, the delusive ego, driven in its ignorance to pursue narrow self-interest at the expense of others.

The strong dominate the weak. Those with political, economic, and military power dominate those who are powerless. Groups and individuals struggle for the control of such power. This is the human story told and retold.

Delusive passions and attachments are embedded so deeply in each of us that they rise endlessly, like weeds, and this is why they are said to be "inexhaustible." To vow to extinguish these seems again like vowing the impossible.

But to actualize this vow we must realize where the root of these delusive passions and attachments lies. To see this root in the blind workings of the ego, which separates and distinguishes my selfish interests from those of others, which puts "my own" welfare above and before that of others, is to see where to attack the problem. In short, uprooting this ego, the source of that delusive distinction between myself and others, the cause of my separation from others, is the key to the extinguishing of the inexhaustible.

The practice of sitting in silence is a concrete way for us to clearly see and then cut through this delusive ego. Practice with the koan Mu is another concrete way toward this. As we deepen our samadhi in just sitting, the delusive ego melts away. To realize mu is to break the chains of the delusive ego and to be opened to a new realm, a new freedom.

A Christian who seeks the will of God in his or her life can be overwhelmed by a realization of his or her own sinfulness, or a sense of unworthiness. Recognizing this can be a mark of honesty and genuine humility in a Christian seeker. But on the other hand, it can result in getting bogged down in our path to God. This sense of sinfulness and unworthiness can be taken in a way that reinforces the notion of separation from God. Conversely, this notion of separation from God aggravates the sense of sinfulness and unworthiness. How then does one break this vicious cycle of separation?

In acknowledging my sinfulness and unworthiness, I am able to entrust my whole (sinful and unworthy) self in the merciful embrace of the Loving God. In other words, in *confessing* my sinfulness and unworthiness, and entrusting myself to God's mercy, I am able to experience this Loving Presence embracing me *just as I am*. Melting in this loving embrace, I am accepted, even in my sinfulness and unworthiness, and I am forgiven. I thereby am able to re-cognize and reclaim my true and original nature "before the foundation of the world—holy and blameless" (Ephesians 1:3) basking in the light of this Loving Presence.

How can this sinful and unworthy being be at the same time holy and blameless? This presents itself to us as another koan. And as a way of approaching this, we can take a verse that is chanted often in many Zen halls called the Verse of Purification:

All harmful karma ever committed by me since of old, on account of my beginningless greed, anger, and ignorance, born of my body, mouth and consciousness, now, I atone it all.

To recognize that I am subject to these delusive passions of greed, anger, and ignorance, is an important facet of my discovery of my True Self. The climactic point of this verse is in the last phrase: *Now,*

I atone it all. Now, in this moment that jumps out of linear time, and touches eternity, I open myself to be at one with it all. And as I realize that I am at one with it all, I am able to live with the consequences of these delusive passions, and take responsibility for them. This is the way to purification. To atone for my delusive passions and its results, as I recognize that I am at one with it all.

GATES OF THE TRUTH ARE COUNTLESS; I VOW TO OPEN THEM

The first part of this third vow proclaims that any and all of the myriad things in the universe can be our gate to enlightenment. By this vow then the seeker after wisdom resolves to open the heart and mind to embrace each and all of the myriad things of the universe as a gate to his or her True Self.

A well-known passage from Zen master Dogen's collection of Zen talks, the *Shobogenzo* (The Eye of the Treasury of True Dharma) gives us a clue to the unraveling of this vow.

> To study the Buddha Way is to study the Self. To study the self is to forget the self. To forget the self is to be enlightened by the myriad things of the universe.

In this verse, what is translated as the English word "study" is the same Chinese/Japanese character in the third vow that is translated as "open." A more literal translation of the vow would be: "Gates to Truth are countless. I vow to study (or learn) them all." Taking the cue from Dogen's passage, then, the seeker may be able to enter a gate to the Truth by considering any particular phenomenon, any one of the countless (myriad) things in the universe. It could be a tree, a mountain, a particle of dust, or the chirping of a bird, the bark of a dog. Or it could be one's own breathing. It could even be a tragic event like the death of a loved one. In other words, any one of these myriad things could be one's gate to enlightenment. But to open and enter any of these gates to enlightenment involves a total dissolution of one's conception of a self separate from these myriad things. In technical terms, this is the dissolution of the subject-object dichotomy that characterizes our ordinary consciousness. As this dichotomy is overcome, with the dissolution of the "perceiving subject," lo and behold, the "perceived object" (tree, mountain, etc.) also ceases to be such. What happens then? This is the moment that the Buddha Way comes to be fully manifest.

From a Christian context, the Ignatian phrase "Finding God in all things" appears to resonate with the intent of this third vow. One of the highlights of the Spiritual Exercises of Saint Ignatius is an exercise that is known as the Contemplation on Divine Love. This is offered to the practitioner toward the culmination of the process of Spiritual Exercises after he or she has gone through the arduous stages of purification of sins and tendencies to separate from God's will, and of illumination into the ways of God's action in history, through the contemplation of the life, death, and resurrection of Jesus Christ, the Holy One of God. At this stage the practitioner is fully disposed to live his or her life in conformity with the will of the Loving God. This exercise invites the practitioner to consider elements of creation, beginning with inanimate objects like rocks and pebbles, continuing with vegetation, and then on to animal life and humans.

Taking a pebble in one's hand, for example, feeling its texture, throwing it up in the air and catching it again (noting the phenomenon known as "gravity" that brings it back to my hand), considering the fact that "it exists," can be a gateway to a deep experience of the Mystery of Being. Or one can gaze at a flower, as many poets have, and perhaps encounter the realm that William Blake articulated in his poem:

To see the world in a grain of sand
And heaven in a wild flow'r.
To hold infinity in the palm of your hand
And eternity in an hour.

This third vow also reminds us of the fact that here are so many things to be learned and mastered in one's search for wisdom. The rudiments of sitting, the introductory elements are but the prelude toward a treasure house of inexhaustible learning. And each step in the process introduces the next one, and one is ever filled with wonder as one proceeds on within the labyrinth, circling on toward the center.

In those Zen lineages using koans, those who have broken through the initial barrier and are confirmed to have glimpsed that world of Emptiness in a "breakthrough" experience will be confronted anew with koan after koan, as another gate to be opened and entered. Each koan presents a shining aspect of a multifaceted and multilayered crystal. One infinite crystal all in all, but with an inexhaustible measure of gleaming facets to behold, one after another.

If we gaze at even one facet and are able to penetrate through it, thus making it our very own, we acquire the master key to opening all the others. We also realize that each facet reflects none other than our very own original face.

Once an initial gate is opened in this realm of boundless gates to the Truth, we proceed, going deeper and deeper, approaching it from an infinite number of angles. A Japanese saying goes: "There is always something higher, something deeper," a journey to the infinite, but whereby each step presents the fullness of infinity in itself.

A Christian writer of the early centuries, Gregory of Nyssa, had an expression that somehow captures this marvelous journey of opening gate after gate that reveals more of that unfathomable Truth, when he noted that our ultimate destiny, that is, union with the Infinite Truth that is God, is a journey that takes us "from glory to glory."

THE ENLIGHTENED WAY IS UNSURPASSABLE;
I VOW TO EMBODY IT

The vow to accomplish the peerless, unsurpassable way of enlightenment is simply the vow to realize one's very own True Self. We are not in search of something out there beyond our present reach. We are not on a journey toward some place far off.

Consider this passage from T. S. Eliot's *Four Quartets:*

We shall not cease from exploration
And the end of all our exploring

Will be to arrive where we started
And know the place for the first time.

It is right before us, *here, now,* but to get to this place we must embark on an endless and perilous journey. It is endless because there is no stopping. To arrive does not mean to cease from further proceeding, because there are always greater depths to be fathomed. It is perilous, because there are many obstacles and pitfalls in the process. The delusive ego lurks at every corner, waiting to catch us unaware.

But Zen Master Dogen's hint, from the passage cited above, related to the third vow, is precious. The practice of sitting in silence, and experiencing *just sitting,* is a practice of self-forgetting. Similarly, the practice of the koan Mu is a practice of self-forgetting. In Zen practice, one learns to abandon oneself in every breath. For those practicing with the koan Mu, one learns to abandon oneself and surrender to Mu, and only Mu. What else is there? There is only an abandonment of oneself in the present moment, in the present endeavor. To forget oneself is simply to abandon oneself in this way to whatever one is doing, wherever one is, in each situation one is placed.

The unsurpassable Way of Enlightenment, may lead one through the dark night of the soul. This is a stage in the journey to God as mapped out by Saint John of the Cross, where there is nothing before us but darkness, darkness, darkness. Persisting in our sitting practice through these times when we feel no trace of spiritual consolation can be a toilsome, irksome, painful process, an excruciating experience. But our persistence will eventually yield its fruit. At the end of the tunnel, it is crystal clear snow country, gleaming at every instant, the whole universe embraced!

This "enlightened way" is not referring here to an abstract idea of the universe, but to the very warp and woof of our daily life. Every step, every word, every glance, every smile at each chance encounter, the morning coffee, the letter to be written, the floor to be swept, the voices of the children playing in the streets.

A koan from the *Gateless Gate* may help us here. It is titled "Ordinary Mind Is the Way."

Chao-chou asked Nan-chuan, "What is the Way?"
"Ordinary Mind is the Way," Nan-chuan replied.
Chao-chou asked, "Shall I strive to seek after it?"
"If you strive for it, you will become separated from it,"
   responded Nan-chuan.
"How can I know the Way unless I strive for it?" persisted
Chao-chou.
"The way does not belong to knowing or not knowing. Know
   ing is delusion, not knowing is confusion. When you have
   really reached the true Way beyond doubt, you will find it as
   vast and boundless as outer space. How can you talk about it
   on the level of right and wrong?"
With these words, Chao-chou instantly attained realization.

In the Christian tradition, as we look at the lives of the saints, and
see through the embellishments and idealizations that hagiographi-
cal accounts provide, we are struck by the very ordinariness of their
lives. They also woke up in the morning, relieved themselves,
washed their face, ate breakfast, went about their daily tasks, got
tired, got hungry, took their supper, went to bed. Human, all too
human. And we find it hard to believe what the masters of the spiritual life tell us, that this is the stuff that makes for the way of the
saints, the same "ordinary" stuff that makes up our own lives.

As the eyes of our hearts are opened to the Loving Presence that
embraces each and every thing in the universe, in which our entire
being is immersed from moment to moment, we return to where we
have always been—namely, at home in this ordinariness, an unsurpassable mystery—and know it for the very first time.

When we chant these four vows, we may also receive a glimpse of
this unsurpassable Way, as we go beyond striving and not striving,
knowing and not knowing, and abandon ourselves totally in the act
of chanting.

Sentient beings are numberless; I vow to free them.
Delusions are inexhaustible; I vow to end them.
The gates of Truth are countless; I vow to open them.
The enlightened way is unsurpassable; I vow to embody it.

Kuan-Yin with
a Thousand Hands

WHY ARE SO MANY SPIRITUAL SEEKERS and devout religious practitioners not concerned with problems of society, issues of justice, with the ecological crisis facing us as a global community? Indeed, why do so many, and not only the so-called spiritual seekers, show lack of concern for problems of society and issues of justice, and with the state of our Earth?

It is precisely this lack of concern, one could dare say, that is *causing* the myriad problems of society, all the situations of exploitation and oppression and injustice. Indifference to such problems enables the forces of greed, ignorance, and ego-attachment, individual as well as corporate and collective, to hold their sway and wreak havoc on our planet. Countless victims lose their lives daily, many others continue to live exploited and dehumanized, while many just go on leading lives centered on their own narrow little selves or their narrow little circles of concern—"my career" or "my success" or "my family"; or perhaps "my enlightenment," or "my salvation" or "my religious mission."

As long as enlightenment or salvation or even religious mission remains confined within the boundaries of the individual or collective ego, there remains a divisive factor in one's life that simply compounds all the problems.

If one turns to Zen mainly for "my own peace of mind" or "my own enlightenment," unless there is a radical overturning of this attitude somewhere along the way, one's practice of Zen itself becomes nothing more than a glorified form of ego-centered activity, and therefore something delusive and divisive.

Recently I met an American contemplative Christian monk who told me that before he entered the monastery he was a student activist who gave his all to the peace movement during student protests in the sixties in the United States. Then he realized that he was going in circles and getting nowhere and burning himself out, and that is when he decided to enter the monastery to become a contemplative. He added that he feels he is now making his contribution to peace precisely by being a contemplative, by being faithful to the religious life and praying for peace and for justice.

I mentioned this in conversation to Brother David Steindl-Rast, who is himself a contemplative monk in the Benedictine order, and who also is quite an active participant in peace movements, finding himself often in the forefront of human rights activities and anti-nuclear protests. I asked for his view on the matter. Let me summarize briefly what came out of a long conversation with Brother David, who for me remains a source of inspiration and an embodiment of enlightenment.

Brother David said that it is true that one can participate in peace movements, human rights activities, and so on, perhaps with a great amount of social concern and interest in the well-being of others, but this participation can be mingled also with some kind of self-righteousness or even some self-centered motivation, or with one's own anger and frustration at the way things are in society. In such a case one constantly needs to be purified of these elements in order that actions and ways of relating with others not be destructive and divisive. A sensitive and sincere social activist realizes this need of purification and can and ought to turn to contemplation and prayer in this context.

Further, the contemplative vocation belongs to a hallowed tradition not only in Christianity, but in Buddhism and in practically all the other major religions as well, and the full and real contribution of these holy men and women who have devoted their lives to prayer and contemplation cannot be measured and exactly quantified.

However, Brother David notes, we can also become *attached* to our prayer and contemplation and thus possibly fail to open ourselves to what God demands in a particular situation. "Go away, don't bother me; I am in contemplation," we might say to God, when God appears in the form of a person knocking at our door asking for a drink of water or for a signature on a petition. We can *institutionalize* our prayer and contemplation and let them become another attachment rather than something that liberates.

The fruits of genuine contemplation, on the other hand, can precisely enable one to be totally free of all ego-attachments, to become a more viable and effective instrument of peace. This is especially so for Christians who are members of various religious orders, as they are freed from family and from financial concerns and are enabled to be a little bit more "agile" than others. Thus, Brother David continues, since he does not have to worry about a family or his job or his reputation, he is totally free to put himself in the forefront of a peace demonstration or an antinuclear sit-in with no fear of the consequences being arrested: "I can pray and contemplate as well in jail as in a monastery cell, or better, even."

At an international religious conference in the United States, I once joined a *vipassana* meditation session conducted by a certain Theravadan Buddhist monk. The meditation theme was on generating loving-kindness or friendliness *(metta)* toward all living beings. As the monk launched us off to a good start in paying attention to our breathing, he went on to suggest evoking a feeling of friendliness first toward one's body, part by part, from the foot to the head, and then toward other persons that came to mind, and then toward a wider and wider field, to include all living beings in the whole world, desiring their happiness and well-being.

The first part of the meditation went off rather well, and then our director-monk continued by suggesting that we concentrate on some pain we may have, say a pain in the leg or in the back: just to *be aware* of that pain, without attaching any value judgments or desires such as "I want that pain to disappear." After a while we will be able to accept the pain as simply pain, and be able to live with it and no longer consider it *suffering,* he explained. In other words, if one does not associate such ideas as "pain is undesirable" or "I want relief," judgments already based on ego attachment, with the bare and "neutral" fact of the pain itself, then pain ceases to be suffering, and is revealed as mere experience.

This Theravada monk then gave us a concrete example of how meditation can calm us down, give us peace of mind and friendly and compassionate feelings toward all living beings in the universe. However, after the session I was overcome by a nagging doubt, and I regret not having had the opportunity to question the monk about it. The question that lingered on in my mind was this: If this kind of meditation produces that kind of effect of calming us down, making us able to accept things as they are without injecting our ego-centered desires, well and good—but does it not also make us numb to the real suffering of others, the poor, the hungry, the exploited, the victims of structural and actual violence in this world of ours? Are we just dismissing them by simply having "friendly feelings" and "wishes for the well-being" of actual sufferers, from a conjured euphoric state of "contemplativeness"? In other words, does not this kind of practice tend to extinguish that passion for justice, that rightful indignation at the suffering of fellow living beings, and thus become like cold water thrown onto the fire whereby Jesus wanted to set the whole world aflame?

As if to confirm my suspicions, I heard later that the monk who had directed this meditation session just described, though admired and looked up to by many for his unquestionable self-discipline and for his kindness and gentleness in dealing with those around him, was criticized at another religious meeting for lack of interest and sensitivity to certain social issues that naturally should have concerned anyone living in the area where his temple was located.

But, fortunately, a second Theravada monk I met in Thailand quelled my incipient disillusionment with *vipassana* meditation practice:

I met this second monk as (again) I joined a *vipassana* meditation session he was conducting for a group of student activists and social workers from Bangkok. Not yet quite forty years old, he related how he himself had been a student leader during the tumultuous years in Bangkok in the early seventies. He came to a point where he wanted to give himself totally to the people in the best way he could, and he was faced with a decision of whether to go to the hills to join the communist guerrillas or to become a Buddhist monk. He chose the latter, became a disciple of the well-known monk Buddhadasa Bhikku, who lives in the southern part of Thailand in semi-contemplation and welcomes anyone who would care to come for *vipassana* meditation with him. At that point, when I met him, after many years of practice himself, he was able to direct others in meditation and had written several books in the Thai language on questions of meditation and social involvement.

"My hope is, on the one hand, to be able to get my activist friends in the slums of Bangkok and in the countryside to do vipassana, and on the other, to get my fellow monks to go out to the slums and to the farms to meet the people there and know their situation." And so he is doing just that, directing *vipassana* sessions especially for those involved in tasks of social change, and getting monks out to the slums and to the impoverished farm to meet people who are concerned and involved in those tasks of social action, so that there can be a stimulating exchange.

This second monk was himself quite active in providing support for a Buddhist-Christian center for development in Bangkok and, together with those working in this center, envisions a future for the Thai people that hopefully will enable them to ward off the destructive effects of Western consumerism by going back to their own cultural and religious roots, back to the basic values presented by Buddhism with regard to respect for life, respect for nature.

For this second monk, meditation practice, far from numbing him to the real suffering and pain of others, heightens his awareness of these realities and provides the inner dynamism for him to continue in his manifold tasks in the reconstruction of society.

So, what makes the difference between a meditative or contemplative practice that makes people turn within themselves in a self-contented and semi-euphoric state, and one that makes them more sensitive to the reality of pain and suffering in the world and to their place in that very pain and suffering, and thus spurs them to deeper involvement in the social dimension?

Let me answer from a Zen perspective:

I have mentioned that there are three fruits of Zen practice: (1) the development of the power of concentration, (2) the attainment of self-realization or enlightenment, and (3) the actualization or personalization of this enlightenment in every aspect and every dimension of one's total being and in one's everyday life. Now if one takes the first fruit and centers one's Zen on the development of the power of concentration, one can indeed after a time notice the change in one's perception of things. As a natural result of sitting efforts and efforts at awareness, one is more able to have a sense of wholeness in one's life, to have a wholesome feeling in day-to-day existence, and to appreciate the little things that go on around one, to even be more gentle and kind and friendly toward all beings that come one's way.

But without the realization of the second fruit, all these "natural results" of one's sitting efforts still leave one unsettled about the basic questions of existence, the basic questions of life and death. *Who am I? What is my ultimate destiny? How am I to relate to my neighbor, to the world?* Such questions remain unanswered and are not solved by concentration alone.

It is the realization of one's True Self, that flash of seeing into one's original nature, that truly liberates one from that basic ego-centeredness, and leads to realizing the empty nature of all things and the interconnectedness of all things in their emptiness. It is this realization that truly settles one's mind and heart, one's total being, that frees one from the fear of death and from the attachment to life. And it is this same experience whereby I am able to see the true basis of my relationship to my neighbor, to society, to the whole world.

In Christian terminology this enlightenment experience is the realization of one's being "embedded" in the whole Body of Christ:

"This is My Body, which is to be given up for you" (Luke 22:19). And thus, "We, though many, are one body in Christ, and we are individually members of one and other" (Romans 12:5). It is not just a "logical consequence" that I become involved in the suffering of others, but an *unavoidable inner exigency;* it is my own pain!

This oneness with all living beings in all their "joys and hopes, griefs and anxieties," especially with "those who are poor or in any way afflicted" *(Gaudium et Spes, No. 1, Documents of the Second Vatican Council)* is not just a pious platitude, but constitutes a central aspect of one's mode of being, permeating every aspect of one's daily life.

Thus the third fruit of Zen consists in the process of letting this realization permeate one's total existence. As mentioned before, the practice of just sitting, as well as koan practice, are geared toward this permeation.

Regarding the latter, each koan deals with a concrete and particular facet of existence that brings one back to the roots of the experience of enlightenment. Through the koan we are invited to *actually* experience my oneness in being with, say, a dog, a cat, a cow, or the stars in heaven, a running stream, a mountain. But let me stop here lest I reveal too much of what goes on in the interview room with the Zen master. The point is that koan exercise in Zen polishes the inner eye to enable us to become intimately united with every situation encountered, and to be able to respond to that situation, not based on some thought or ideology or some calculated set of norms, but from a direct perception in the source of my very being in a way that is demanded by the situation. As Gospels put it: "I was hungry, and you gave me to eat, I was thirsty, you gave me to drink, I was a stranger, and you welcomed me" (Matthew 25:35)

Such a way of responding to every situation in daily life is pictured for us in the image of Kuan-Yin with a Thousand Hands. Kuan-Yin, called Kannon or Kanzeon in Japanese (literally meaning "Perceiver of the Cries of the World") is the bodhisattva *par excellence* in Buddhism, who in her enlightened state perceives the emptiness of all existence. Incidentally, in the original Sanskrit, Avalokiteshvara is of male gender, but this bodhisattva evolved later in China as an androgynous and eventually a female form, embodying the aspect of compassion that naturally flows out of the wisdom of enlightenment.

The thousand hands of Kuan-Yin represent the way she touches, and responds in myriad compassionate ways, in all kinds of situations in our lives. And if one looks closely, each of the thousand hands is meant to perform a distinct function, such as allaying fear, wiping out evil, fighting enemies of injustice, driving out demons, healing fevers and all kinds of diseases, setting the Dharma wheel in motion, calling forth the inner religious drive in living beings that leads them to see the fleetingness of existence and to seek the wisdom of enlightenment, and many more.

The bodhisattva is also portrayed as having eleven faces, signifying her ability to perceive everything in all directions. In short, in whatever situation of suffering, illness, difficulty, or need living beings find themselves, the bodhisattva "extends a hand" in a way that answers

the call of the situation. "I was hungry and you gave me to eat, thirsty and you gave me to drink, a stranger and you welcomed me."

Kuan-Yin is venerated as an idealized figure and object of devotion by adherents of different Buddhist traditions. In Zen practice communities, devotion is likewise expressed, as we place the figure of Kuan-Yin on elevated platforms, adorning it with flowers, offering incense, and bowing before the figure. But an important reminder is given from the Zen perspective, as we are told that Kuan-Yin is not "out there" on the elevated platform, but that each and every one of us is Kuan-Yin. Our Zen practice is our way of realizing how to be Kuan-Yin, or of actualizing the reality of Kuan-Yin in our own lives.

In the Christian tradition, the figure of Mary, the Mother of Jesus, and thereby, the Mother of God, is likewise revered as an object of devotion in many kinds of ways throughout different cultures. A commonly recited prayer is the Ave Maria, extolling the virtues of Mary and asking for her intercession throughout one's life and especially at the hour of one's death.

Mary is the embodiment of compassion for Christians. There is a poignant scene where she stands at the foot of the Cross of her son Jesus, deep in sorrow and bearing the pain of her own Loved One, memorialized in artistic works, from paintings to poems. The famous sculpture Pieta by Michelangelo also depicts Mary in her sorrow as she carries the lifeless body of Jesus. In short, Mary embodies the Compassion that weeps with all beings in their sorrow, bearing the pain of the world with her son, Jesus.

The Second Vatican Council issued a document on Mary the Mother of Jesus, and while upholding traditional Christian theological doctrines and devotional practices toward Mary, also brought out a very significant feature. In addition to being a figure to be venerated, the document affirms, Mary is to be regarded as the model of all Christians, as embodying the kind of life that each one who regards oneself as a follower of Christ is called to live. In other words, the invitation here, as one reveres the figure of Mary, is likewise, to *be* Mary, to embody in one's life all that Mary signifies.

As the figure of Mary embodies all that a Christian is called to be, Kuan-Yin with a Thousand Hands embodies the mode of being of one who has reached the ultimate fruit in Zen. This is a mode of being that has undergone a total emptying of oneself, leading to one's total liberation, whereby one's whole being is given over for others as they are encountered in their particular situations. "This is my body which is given up for you."

Zen Experience
of Triune Mystery

WE MUST MAKE CLEAR at the outset that zen as such is non-theistic, that is, not at all concerned with the notion of God or with the question of God's existence or nonexistence. Rather, its central concern, as in Buddhism in general, is the resolution of the fundamental problem of human existence, characterized in this tradition as dukkha (dissatisfactoriness).

Our task in this chapter is to listen intently and carefully to what Zen has to offer in terms of its understanding of our *human existence,* and based on such careful listening, we can then offer some reflections on the implications of such an understanding of human existence for those who wish to engage in God-talk, that is, *theo-logy.* I will also briefly summarize some of what I have said regarding Zen in the preceding chapters.

ZEN: THE AWAKENED LIFE

Zen defines itself with a fourfold set of characteristics said to come from Bodhidharma, the wild-eyed and bearded ascetic depicted in many Zen paintings, who brought this way of meditative practice from India to China around the sixth century of our common era. The essence of Zen is presented in the following verse attributed to Bodhidharma:

Not relying on words or letters, (it is)
A special transmission outside of Scriptures,
Pointing directly to the human mind,
Seeing one's nature, being awakened.

It is thus repeatedly emphasized that Zen is not a doctrine or a philosophy that can be presented and accounted for in verbal and conceptual terms, but rather a praxis and way of life centered on the experience of "seeing one's (true) nature," and thereby "being awakened," in other words, becoming a Buddha, or "awakened one."

We can identify three "moments" in this way of life, which we will examine in the three following subsections.

Emptying of ego-consciousness

The crux of this way of life is the practice of seated meditation, or zazen. Zazen is the locus wherein we can uncover all that Zen is about, the fulcrum of an awakened life. It involves sitting (either on a cushion or low chair) with one's back straight, legs folded, eyes open, and in this posture, breathing deeply but regularly, letting one's mind come to rest in the here and now.

Its pivotal point is in the emptying of ego-consciousness, casting off that mode of thinking that divides our being into subject and object, seer and seen, hearer and heard, thinker and thought, self and other, as well as all the other oppositions we find in our life: birth and death, pleasure and pain, good and evil, here and there, now and then. In other words, in zazen, the practitioner enters into a process that culminates in total self-emptying. As one's praxis ripens, the oppositions are overcome, and one arrives at a state of pure awareness *(samadhi)*. Such a state of awareness is also called "nonthinking."

However, this state is not to be mistaken for absent-mindedness, or absolute passivity or loss of consciousness. On the contrary: It is one that involves a total engagement in one's sitting. Consider the following passage, from the writings of Dogen, a Japanese Zen master of the thirteenth century:

> Once, when the Great Master Hung-tao of Yueh-shan was sitting in meditation, a monk asked him, "What are you thinking, sitting there so fixedly?"
> The master answered, "I'm thinking of not thinking."
> The monk asked, "How do you think of not thinking?"
> The master answered, "Nonthinking."

We will not go into the technicalities involved in the longstanding debate on this matter of "nonthinking," and will simply note that it is neither introspection, wherein the subject turns inward but still in a way that thinks of mental objects, nor the stopping of mental faculties. Insightful descriptions of what this involves can be found in a book edited by John Daido Loori, *The Art of Just Sitting: Essential Writings on the Zen Practice of Shikantaza*. In this state of awareness, one overcomes the normal subject-object modal way of thinking, and one arrives at an awareness of pure *be*-ing.

Return to the concrete world

This awareness of pure *be*-ing is not something that happens in a vacuum, but in and through the very concrete historical conditions surrounding one's zazen practice. It is not an "out-of-body" experience, but very much an embodied event rooted in the specific historical realities of one's being. And yet, at this very place, in this very moment, all the boundaries of space and of time collapse, as there is no "subject" standing, or sitting, *vis-à-vis* a given objective place, and no time before or time after that a given subject can measure or tally.

With the emptying of ego-consciousness, the "object" that one is normally conscious of is also emptied, and thus there is no longer anything "out there" to be seen, or heard, or smelled, or tasted, or touched. There is absolutely *"nothing out there"* anymore, and there is "nothing in here" that looks out and sees.

This experience of the emptying of one's ego-consciousness opens out to an entirely *new dimension* about which no verbal description can do justice (i.e., "not relying on words or letters"). Yet again, as noted above, it does not take place in a vacuum or in an extraterrestrial realm but right here and right now. As such, it is an experience that goes full circle in a second "moment," with a recovery of our embodied way of be-ing.

Consider this koan:

> Chao-chou earnestly asked Nanchuan: "What is the Way?"
> Nanchuan answered, "The ordinary mind is the Way."

My Zen teacher, Koun Yamada, says of this koan: "It is nothing but our ordinary everyday life. It is just getting up, washing your face, eating breakfast, going to work, walking, running. laughing, crying; the leaves on the trees, the flowers in the field, whether white, red, or purple. It is birth, it is death. That is the Way"

But there is a difference: It is no longer getting up, washing one's face, and so on, in the way we would do these ordinary actions under the governance of our ego-consciousness. The leaves on the trees, the flowers in the field are no longer "out there" as objects of our consciousness. Rather, all these activities become the consummate expressions of that pure awareness of be-ing, emptied of all ego-consciousness, while being embedded in concrete historical reality.

In short, *objects are emptied of their objectivity,* emptied of the perceiving act, and likewise are experienced as the concrete manifestations of pure fact itself, unobjectified, unsullied, unparalleled, just as they are.

Zen enlightenment thus involves a "moment" of the emptying of ego-consciousness, and a "moment" of return to concrete historical reality. These, however, are not separate events following each in a linear time, but, although distinguishable, can be simultaneous and timeless.

There is a third "moment" that characterizes human existence from the vantage point of the Zen enlightenment experience. This is the aspect that we can only begin to describe as a plunge into the sea of compassion.

Sea of compassion

In the miscellaneous koans of our Sanbo Kyodan tradition, given to a practitioner who has manifested an experience of emptying and of returning to embodied form as summarized above, there is one that goes thus:

> *In the sea of Ise, ten thousand feet down, lies a Stone.*
> *I wish to pick up that stone without wetting my hands.*

This koan can only be solved if one is truly emptied of self, and as one is ready to plunge one's whole being into the depths of that sea of Ise, underneath which that precious stone lies. One who is able to manifest this readiness and is thereby able to plunge into the sea and retrieve this stone "without wetting his or her hands" is told of its two marvelous qualities, which are in fact features of one's own True Self: First, it can never get wet. Second, it can never get dry. Wondrous! Mysterious! The first quality, of never getting wet, refers to that dimension that we can term "impassibility"—— impermeability to any outside influence, to suffering or pain. How is this? It is totally empty! Nothing to wet, nothing outside to get wet with. Realizing this aspect of one's True Self is the key to total liberation from suffering. In Christian tradition, the doctrine of God's impassibility is a fundamental feature in the understanding of the notion of God: God is conceived as the One who is beyond all suffering and pain, unaffected by anything that is not God.

The second quality, which appears to be a direct contradiction of the first, refers to that dimension of com-passion. This marvelous Stone can never get dry, as it is always flowing with tears of compassion, as long as there are sentient beings who are suffering and are struggling with greed, anger, and ignorance, the three poisons that keep us mired in suffering.

The awakened life is thus seen as coming to fruition in a third "moment": The barrier that divides Self and Other having been broken, one awakens as immersed in a bottomless sea of com-passion (literally, "suffering-with"), every single breath finding oneself at-one with all sentient beings in this common lot of sentient beings. This sea of compassion is the matrix that nourishes an awakened one, and empowers him or her to engage in concrete tasks in the historical world.

The Zen way of life and praxis as such does not at all refer in an explicit way to the notion of God, nor does it need this notion in its articulation within the Zen tradition. Our question then is this: What can we learn from the Zen way of life and praxis that can throw light on a possible understanding of Christian existence, wherein the notion of God is indeed so central.

Unknown and unknowable Mystery

The first moment in Zen praxis is the entry into a realm that on the one hand is emptied of the ego as grasping subject. This realm is described as a state of *total blindness* (from the subject point of view), and also as a state of *total darkness* (from the object point of view). It is entry into a realm that is ultimately unknown and unknowable (that is, in so far as "knowledge" implies a grasp of some objective reality by a conscious subject). If God-talk, theology, is to make any sense in this context, it is the affirmation that God as ultimately unknown and unknowable, unobjectifiable, *un-image-able,* and which no verbal description or intellectual formulation can ever approach. It is an unfathomable realm that, in the words of the late spiritual writer Thelma Hall, is "too deep for words"; it is a realm that is, echoing Augustine, "more intimate to me than I am to myself."

Enlightened as a new creation

But if one only dwells in the realm of this first "moment," then one is forever lost in the unknown, unable to see or speak, or even move at all. It is the second "moment" that makes possible the *real-ization,* the "making real," of the Zen experience in the concrete world of human events. Here one comes full circle and returns to the very concreteness of one's embodied being, in the here and now. In other words, the realm of emptiness comes to take a concrete *shape,* whether it be a color such as a brown patch on the wall, or a sound such as the sneeze of someone nearby, the pain in one's legs. In this second "moment," the divine darkness comes to light and manifests itself in the ordinary mind. But there is a difference: One experiences each event, each aspect of one's ordinary life, from its fulcrum in emptiness, that is, as *enlightened* by the divine darkness.

This difference is echoed in Paul's exclamation (in Galatians 2:20) mentioned above: "I live, no longer I but Christ in me." In Pauline terms, plunged into the mystery of Christ's death-resurrection, having died to one's self, one lives in the newness of life, in all that one is and does. Emptied of self, arriving at that realm that is beyond all knowledge, one comes to be filled with the utter fullness of God. Our ultimate destiny is simply "to know the love of Christ which surpasses all knowledge, that we may be filled with the fullness of God" (Ephesians 3:18–19). Everything, every moment, is experienced as a new creation, and in this way, we experience the fullness of this Mystery.

Solidarity in suffering

Next, one awakens in the depths of the sea of com-passion, shared suffering, identifying with the suffering of all sentient beings. In Christian terms, to live the newness of life "in Christ" is also to live as suffering-with all those embraced by Christ on the Cross. Thus, with every breath, as one is filled with the newness of life in Christ, one swims in the sea of com-passion.

One is confirmed in this solidarity with those bearing the wounds of the world in and through the very Breath that empowers us to be one with the pain of all those who suffer. This is a dynamism (a word derived from the Greek word "power") that also moves us in the direction of the healing of all wounds and for reconciliation of all that is separate. This power of com-passion is what moves a person to engage him- or herself in concrete ways toward the alleviation of the world's suffering. It guides us in making concrete decisions to take on the real and difficult tasks in our actual situation.

THE INNER CIRCLE OF MYSTERY

Taken together, the elements of the Zen awakened life open our eyes to a "triune Mystery" that is at the very heart of our human existence.

This Mystery consists, first, in the Unknown and Unknowable, which is also the unfathomable Source of all—"No one has ever seen God…"(John 1:18; 6:46); second, in the One wherein all things come to being, fully manifest and embodied in historical reality—"And the Word became flesh, and dwelt among us" (John 1:14), the Eternal Word in and through whom all myriad things of the universe were made, and "without whom there was not anything that was made" (John 1:3); and third, in the Sea of Compassion in which we are immersed at the heart of our being, identified also as the living Breath that sustains and unites the whole of creation and gives and fills it with life ("The earth was without form, and void…and the Breath of God moved over the waters" (Genesis 1:2); "It is the Breath that gives life" (John 6:63). This is the one and same triune Mystery that is both the ground and the fulfillment of human existence.

One simply awakens to one's True Self as already embedded within the heart of this Mystery: The Unknown, the Manifest, and the Sea of Com-passion. One awakens as already situated at the *inner circle* of its dynamic Life, from Breath to Breath.

In his treatise on the Trinity, Saint Augustine observes:

> But love is of someone that loves, and with love something is loved. Behold, then, there are three things: The One that loves, that which is loved, and Love itself.

In the light of the description of the three "moments" of the Zen experience offered above, we may venture a correlation. The Unknowable Source is the One that loves, the One addressed as Abba, Father and Mother of all. The Manifest is that which is loved, the Eternal Image of that Source, which is also the Firstborn of all creation, and upon whom all the myriad things of the universe are grounded in being. And that Sea of Com-passion is Love itself, the Breath of God which brings together and vivifies the entire universe.

To awaken to one's true nature is to realize oneself as embraced in this dynamic circle of Love. It is to recognize one's True Self at the very bosom of this triune Mystery of Love, in every breath, every step, every moment of one's life.

Zen and Christian Spirituality
ATTUNING TO THE BREATH

POSTURE, BREATHING, AND SILENCING the mind are the three key elements of *zazen* or Zen sitting practice. First, one assumes a bodily position conducive to prolonged stillness, preferably taking a lotus position, but most important, keeping one's back as straight as possible while maintaining the natural curve in the lower back. Second, one regulates the breathing, paying attention with each in-breath and out-breath. Third, one silences the mind by not dwelling on any particular thought or sensation, but by being fully present as one sits, paying attention to every breath.

Now in the Christian tradition, the term spirituality derives from the Greek *pneuma* or spirit, which in turn derives from the Hebrew *ruah,* "the Breath of God." Throughout the Old Testament the Breath of God plays a key function in all the significant events of salvation history, beginning with the act of creation itself as portrayed in Genesis. The Breath of God is the very dynamic presence of God, a presence that gives life to all and renews the face of the earth.

The whole life of Jesus is permeated with this dynamic presence, the Breath of God, from the time of his conception in the womb of the Blessed Mother—"The Holy Spirit will come upon you, and the power of the Most High will overshadow you" (Luke 1:35)— up to the completion of his life on the cross when he gave the Breath back to the Father—"Into Thy hands, I commend my spirit" (John 19:30).

The theme of Jesus' whole life is summarized in the quotation from Isaiah that he read at the synagogue in his hometown of Nazareth:

> The Breath of the Lord is upon me,
> Who has anointed me to preach good news to the poor,
> Sent me to proclaim release to the captives,
> and the recovery of sight to the blind.
> To set at liberty those who are oppressed,
> to proclaim the acceptable year of the Lord.
>
> (Luke 4:18–19)

The key to understanding the life of Jesus is in realizing that he is replete with the Breath of God. His whole existence is vivified, guided, inspired by and fulfilled in it. Jesus was confirmed in this identity, as he heard the voice while he was being baptized in the river Jordan: "You are my Beloved, in whom I am well pleased" (Mark 1:11).

For Christians, spirituality is nothing other than a life in attunement to the Spirit, the Breath of God, wherein one lets one's total being be taken up in its dynamic presence, be guided by it in reading the signs of the times and in responding to every situation. In entrusting oneself to the Breath of God, one is also able, in moments of grace, to hear that affirming word: You are my Beloved, in whom I am well pleased.

Paying attention to one's breathing in Zen, then, is not simply a physical exercise that keeps one concentrated on one point, but the very abandonment of one's total being to the Breath of God, here and now. It is letting one's whole self be possessed by the Breath of God, to be vivified, guided, inspired and fulfilled in it.

And as one is subsumed by the Spirit, the Breath of God, one's whole being becomes offered for this divine and dynamic liberating action in history: To preach good news to the poor, to proclaim release to the captives, to liberate the oppressed.

But one must ask concretely, *Who are the poor, the captives, the oppressed?* The answer can only come from a reading of the concrete situation of the world today, in other words, an actual exposure to the situations of poverty, oppression, exploitation, and ecological destruction that many living beings are trapped in today. To place oneself on the side of the victims of the structural and actual violence that is going on in today's world will provide us the key to answer this question. And only if we are able to recognize, in the concrete, the poor, the captives, the oppressed, the marginalized, will we be able to ask the next set of questions: What is the nature of the *good news* that is to be preached to the poor? the *release* to be proclaimed to the captives? the *liberty* to be realized for the oppressed?

In order to tackle this second set of questions, one cannot remain on a naive level of simply responding superficially to each situation as it arises, of treating every pain with a mere external remedy. Rather, a total healing calls for an examination of the *causes* of the sickness, and the taking of steps to enable the whole organism to move on the way to recovery. We need sophisticated methods of socioeconomic analysis as well as thorough ecological assessment of our present contemporary world situation, from all its different angles. Based on this, we can thus move in the direction of projects and programs that respond to the needs brought to light through this socio-economic analysis and assessment.

But the point here is, whatever follows in the light of such analysis as the desirable modes of action to be taken in responding to the given situations, these are all done simply as one's response to the call of the Breath upon which one has entrusted one's whole existence.

Thus the concrete steps to be taken as one surrenders one's being to the liberating divine action in history are simply natural movements taken based on attuning oneself to the Breath, letting oneself be totally possessed by it; here and now, with every in-breath, out-breath, responding to the concrete tasks of each given situation.

An awakened person, made aware of his or her total nothingness, yet at the same time called out of this nothingness to the fullness of being by the Infinite source of life, can perhaps sum up his or her whole existence in two short passages: "You are my Beloved, in whom I am well pleased" (Mark 1:11). Grounded in this affirming Love, one thus exclaims, "The Breath of the Lord is upon me"(Luke 4:16).

Appendix

*Conversations with Koun Yamada Roshi
and Father Hugo Enomiya-Lassalle*

INTRODUCTORY NOTE

Koun Yamada Roshi (1907–1989) was Zen master of San-un Zendo, or the Zen Hall of the Three Clouds, located in Kamakura, Japan. Since the late 1960s, after Yamada Roshi took over the leadership of the Sanbo Kyodan Zen lineage from the late Yasutani Hakuun Roshi (1885–1973), many Christians, including lay Catholics, as well as priests, sisters, seminarians, and Protestant ministers and laypersons, began to practice Zen with him, joining the numerous Buddhist practitioners already under his guidance. Many of these are now directing others in Zen practice in the United States, Europe, and Asia. His commentary on the famous koan collection called *Wumen-kuan* was published in English under the title *The Gateless Gate*.

Father Hugo Enomiya-Lassalle, S.J. (1898–1990) was a German-born Jesuit priest who had lived in Japan since 1929. He started practicing

Zen meditation "to learn more about Japanese culture," according to his own account, and wrote many books about his experiences. After receiving training from several different Zen masters, in the early 1970s he came in contact with Koun Yamada Roshi, under whose guidance he completed koan training, and by whom he was authorized himself as Zen teacher. It was Father Lassalle's pioneering efforts in directing Zen retreats in Europe that enabled many Western Christians to see the possibilities of deepening their spiritual life in the practice of Zen.

I was privileged to have been able to receive the guidance of these two spiritual giants whose influence will continue to be felt long after their time.

The conversation recorded below took place in Japan in the late 1980s shortly before these two great teachers died. It was in the late sixties and early seventies that an increasing number of Christians, both religious and lay, began to gather around as Zen disciples of Koun Yamada Roshi in Kamakura. It was indeed a very rare opportunity in those days to have a Zen meditation retreat, a *sesshin,* under the direction of an authentic Buddhist Zen master participated in by both Buddhists and Christians. At dawn, while the Buddhists chanted their sutras, the Christians gathered in another room of the Zen Hall to celebrate the Eucharist. Other than during this particular period, everything else was done together without distinction—a true sharing of life, on the part of both groups. I was still in my studies in the Jesuit seminary, and Father Lassalle, being the only priest at that time, would be the celebrant at the Eucharist.

Such a "dialogue of life" has been made possible by the great vision of Yamada Roshi, wherein now Buddhists and Christians transcend their sectarian boundaries and share in the same life of Zen. This is certainly evidence of a new consciousness arising that is grounded on their Zen experience.

Ruben Habito: What particular points do you keep in mind as you direct Christians in the Zen practice?

Yamada Roshi: Naturally one of the very first questions many Christians ask me is whether they can remain faithful Christians in coming to practice Zen—and I always answer them that they need not worry about forsaking or losing their Christianity. Zen is not a religion in the sense of a system of beliefs and concepts and practices that demands exclusive allegiance, and they do not have to think of it as such. Zen is something other than that, and so I can tell Christians that they do not have to throw away their Christianity as they come to Zen. What Zen is, and how it is different from Christianity as I see it, I will not speak of right now.

RH: Father Lassalle, I understand that you had already been in Japan for a good number of years and had played an important role in the building of the Japanese mission of the Society of Jesus even before the outbreak of the Second World War. It was in this context that you came to some Buddhist teachers for instruction in Zen. What led you to the practice of Zen?

Father Lassalle: When I was a young Jesuit doing my studies for the priesthood in Germany, I volunteered for the missions. I was impressed by the challenge in Africa, especially how people were living under very strict conditions of poverty, and how there were still slaves, and so forth, and I read a book entitled *From Cape Town to Zambesi* about some Jesuits who took a journey on an ox cart. I was in my second year of novitiate, and the German province was then entrusted with the Japanese mission when I wrote my letter volunteering for Africa. So I received an answer directly from Father General saying that it was not the will of God that I go to Africa— and thanking me for volunteering for Japan! So that is how I found myself being assigned to Japan.

RH: What an interesting twist of providence!

Father Lassalle: That is the story of my communication with Father General! And I said to myself that if I am to go to Japan, I must learn about the culture there. It was at that time that I started reading the books written by D. T. Suzuki and learned that Zen had a profound influence on Japanese culture, and was thus convinced that if I wanted to learn about the Japanese mentality I also must learn about Zen. When I came to Japan in 1929, I started to sit zazen on my own, without any instruction. Then I started visiting some

Zen monasteries and received some directions. After that we had a group that practiced Zen sitting, after I was assigned to Hiroshima. In Tsuwano there was a Soto Zen monastery, where I did my first Zen *sesshin*. I was Superior of the Jesuit Missions at that time.

RH: How did the other Jesuits react to your going to a Buddhist monastery to practice Zen?

Father Lassalle: I remember a priest who was worried about me and warned me that if I continued such practices I might lose my faith. And there was a brother who kept murmuring, "What is this Father Lassalle up to now, going to the Buddhists and all?"

RH: How would you describe the experience of your first *sesshin?*

Father Lassalle: At that time, I got such a deep impression that I wondered if we could not adapt these practices among Christians. So I gave a talk to some sisters and encouraged them in the ways of meditation that I learned from Zen. Then I organized a group of Japanese Christians to sit together in the Zen manner, and they were very happy, for they told me that they thought since they had become Christians they were not allowed to do such practices! So I was encouraged, and we continued sitting together regularly; we were even able to build a Zen hall of our own in Kabe, near Hiroshima. Unfortunately the building had to be torn down after the war because the local government needed a place to build a pump for electricity, and though they offered to find another place for me, the Society did not want me to build another hall.

RH: When did you start practicing Zen with Harada Sogaku Roshi?

Father Lassalle: That was after the war. There were many things destroyed by the war, and we were engaged in the process of rebuilding. So for a while I was busy as Jesuit Superior in building the memorial cathedral in Hiroshima. But when that was finished I made a fresh start with Zen and inquired at Eiheiji, the central temple of the Soto Sect, and they recommended that I go to Harada Roshi. When I eventually told Harada Roshi, he was quite surprised because at that time he was not in good standing with the Eiheiji people. I was with him for about five or six years and received the Mu koan from Harada Roshi. After he died I tried to continue with his successors in the temple, but did not get too far. So it was after a while that I went to Koun Yamada Roshi for direction, and that is where I am now.

☾

Yamada Roshi: There are some questions I would like to ask Christians who come to me for direction in Zen. I have been wanting to ask these questions for a long time now, but I have kept them to myself, as I felt these may just confuse Christians as they begin their Zen practice. But I feel confident I can ask these of both of you now. First, why did you not just continue doing meditational practices following your own Christian tradition instead of coming to Zen? Was there something lacking in Christianity that led you to seek something in Zen, or did you have some dissatisfaction with Christianity that led you to Zen? And also a question to Christians who have had the Zen experience through the Mu koan: How would you express this experience in your own Christian terms? And a third question: After a student has some insight into Mu, there is a koan that asks, "What is the origin of Mu?"…How would you answer a question about the origin of God?

Father Lassalle: For me it was not a question of something lacking in Christianity, but that I wanted to learn more about the Japanese mentality. I wanted to go deeper into the culture and spiritual treasure of the people I have been called to be with. That is why I began the practice of Zen. And as far as the continuance of practices of Christian tradition, it was actually my contact with Zen that enabled me to appreciate better the wealth that is found in Christian tradition, especially the mystical tradition in Europe, including the German and the Spanish mystics. I have written about this in my books about Christian spirituality in encounter with Zen mysticism.

RH: For me it was an attempt to learn from another tradition that led me to Zen in the first place. I first joined a Rinzai Zen *sesshin* soon after coming to Japan, and it left such a deep impression on me that I naturally wanted to go on, and that was when I was introduced to your Zen group. Of course I began Zen with the motivation of delving deeper into the question *Who am I?* This I think puts us at the roots of the matter, the rock-bottom starting point for anyone starting Zen.

However, having already been through the experience of a Jesuit novitiate, including the month-long spiritual exercises of Saint

Ignatius, I could say I was not starting from scratch. I had already gone though a somewhat rough period of self-searching and God-searching in my late teens, ever since my university days in the Philippines, and so all this was behind me when I started Zen. So for me the Mu experience had been prepared for by several stages of believing, doubting, understanding a little, doubting again, and so forth.

When I look at the diary I was writing in those days I am amazed at the various turns and crossroads I was passing through. But anyway, for me the Mu experience, triggered by my working on the koan of Chao-chou's dog, literally shook me inside out, and kept me laughing and even crying for about three days, as I remember. People around me must have thought I was going crazy then. I can only say at this point that the experience enabled me to see the truth, the forcefulness, the real reality of what Paul wanted to express in Galatians 2:20—"It is now no longer I that live, but Christ in me!"

So to answer Yamada Roshi's first and second question in the same breath, I came to Zen in the search for my True Self, and the experience that you certified as *kensho* triggered by the koan Mu was at the same time the realization of my total nothingness. And yet from another angle the experience of this total nothingness is also the discovery of an exhilarating world of the fullness of grace surpassing all expectations. One can only exclaim again with Paul, "Who can fathom the breadth and length and height and depth," and who can "know the love of Christ which surpasses all knowledge"? (Ephesians 3:18–19).

If you ask the origin of all this, I can only admit that I don't know. One can only humbly receive, from moment to moment, the fullness of grace.

Yamada Roshi: I see. I have always accepted Christians as disciples with the implicit understanding that there is something in common that can be shared with them from a Zen perspective, although I do not know much about Christianity as such. However, it seems to me from what I learn from those Christians I have come in contact with that Christianity itself has changed over the years. Or maybe I have had a sort of different idea of Christianity before, and it is that idea that has changed.

RH: Well, yes and no. Before the Second Vatican Council, held from 1962 to 1965, there were certain fixed notions associated with Christianity giving the image of a rigid, closed, and dogmatic set of beliefs backed by highly abstract theological speculations, and linked with a moralistic stance on the world often accompanied by a "holier than thou" attitude toward other persons. Christians also gave the impression that they had a monopoly on the Truth and even held on to the notion that there was "no salvation outside the Church."

Fortunately, or should we say through the work of grace, the Second Vatican Council encouraged a "return to the wellsprings" *(ad fontes)* of Christianity, leading to the further exploration of the experiential roots of the Christian message as expressed in the scriptures. So now we are able to take Christianity as a message of Total Liberation, grounded on an encounter with the divine mystery in and through the humanity of Jesus the Christ. Christianity ultimately boils down to this basic religious experience of encounter of "divinity-in-humanity."

Yamada Roshi: Recently one of my disciples, a Benedictine nun, presented to me a book written by a German Catholic priest, Hans Waldenfels, S.J., with the title *Absolute Nothingness.* I was very much impressed with the contents of the book, and it led me to see that what you Christians call God may not be too different from what we are talking about in Zen. Just the other day I had a meeting with four Catholic priests who have finished the Zen koan training, and during our free discussion I asked them about this, and all of them seemed to agree on the common ground of what you call God and what we are concerned with in Zen. Father Lassalle came later, and he also shared the same view.

RH: Yes, we are now dealing with something that cannot be adequately captured by words and concepts, and if we see things in this perspective, that is, the limitations of the words and concepts that we are using in our dialogue with each other, and are able to see beyond these limitations, then we are able to partake of that sense of communality, that we are breathing the same air and living in the same world.

It seems we have to overcome our one-sided ideas of God as a Superperson up there somehow like a Grandfather in the Sky with a white beard, watching everything, and also understand that God is

No-Person, the ground of all things. Here we are dealing with two concepts, *person* and *no-person* but we have also to deny them both. We have to keep coming back to the experiential ground of our theological language.

☾

Yamada Roshi: I understand that the pope as the head of the Roman Catholic Church is quite concerned with the salvation of humankind, and I admire him for this. But I can say that it is not just the efforts of the pope alone that can save humankind. We must all join hands in our common effort. Zen and Christianity can join hands, and we can be together in this common goal.

And to me, one of the major tasks facing humankind in this day and age is the problem of poverty, or rather the solution to the problem of the poverty of many people here on earth today. This cannot be accomplished by the United Nations alone, or by the Vatican alone. This may be a task that will take us a hundred or two hundred years.

RH: But this question brings us to the issue of the relation of Zen to our historical and social realities. How would you look at the nature of our involvement with the world? This is the very important question of the relation of Zen practice to social action.

Yamada Roshi: If people are hungry, the first thing is to enable them to eat. In such a situation they are in no position to listen to anything else, much less to talk about Zen or Christianity. One must first of all be able to partake of the minimum necessities of life to be able to proceed from there. But again, it is not good to live in luxury. I always stress the way of simplicity, of being content with what is given. Unfortunately, in recent times young people have become too used to and attached to comfort and luxury. This was not the case when we were young.

RH: Father Lassalle, how do you view this question of Zen practice and social involvement?

Father Lassalle: I see it in terms of the coming about of a new consciousness for humankind. This new consciousness transcends the traditional way of looking based on the subject-object polarity that treats others as "objects" confronted by me as a "subject." This new consciousness goes beyond this opposition, and there comes with it an awareness of being one with all. It is this new consciousness that will become the basis of a person's social relations and way of involvement with society.

RH: I would like to consider a little more what Father Lassalle here calls the emerging "new consciousness." There is the case of the individual who is only aware of his or her "subjective consciousness," and thus relates with others, with nature, and so on, in oppositional terms. He or she only sees a very limited area of reality from this vantage point. This is like the visible part of the iceberg. But actually the True Self goes much, much deeper. First, there is the area of the subconscious, activated during sleep, during dreams. Then there is a deeper area of what Carl Jung called the collective unconscious, which is shared by human beings throughout history, as evidenced in common patterns in myths, symbols, archetypes. But even this area does not yet touch what Yamada Roshi would call the "essential world" in Zen. It is what we can call the "phenomenal self."

The breakthrough beyond the subjective consciousness, going deeper than even the subconscious and the collective unconscious, through that realm where opposites coincide, where there is no longer subject or object—the world of emptiness—is our experience of Mu in Zen. This is where one awakens to the basic fact of being one with the whole universe, as well as with each and every particular thing at hand, like this flower, that mountain, the sun, the moon, the stars. It's none other than myself! This is what enabled the Buddha to exclaim, "Above the heavens, beneath the heavens, no other one to be revered but I!"

If this statement is misunderstood, it can be read as the height of blasphemy and egocentricity, but understood properly it is an exclamation of the world of emptiness that is also the world of oneness with every particular thing in this whole universe. There is no other than I, and there is no such I! A conceptual contradiction indeed, but there is no other way to express it.

And from this perspective, where everything becomes manifest "as it truly is," everything is seen with the Eye of Wisdom. It is in the light of this Eye of Wisdom that true compassion arises, for all the pains, the joys, the sufferings, the cries of everyone in the universe are as such my own pain, my joy, my suffering, my cry. It is only from this perspective that genuine works of compassion can come forth. It is not at all like that shallow kind of "pity" for others where one looks at those in suffering as it were from a perspective outside of that suffering. Here in the world of emptiness one is plunged right into that suffering as one's very own.

A straightforward look at our present world as it is will manifest the state of suffering of countless living beings, those suffering in the midst of dehumanizing poverty, where malnourished babies die every minute, and where many continue to die victims of violence both individual and structural. All this is *my very own* suffering, and my body is wracked with pain from all sides. I cannot remain complacent and unconcerned. I am inspired by an inner dynamism to be involved in the alleviation of this pain and suffering, in whatever capacity I am able. I am reminded of the image of the goddess of mercy, the bodhisattva Kwan-Yin with a thousand hands, reaching out all over the world to those who are suffering.

RH: What do you each see as the tasks for the Zen-Christian dialogue in the future?

Father Lassalle: I would like to quote Jean Gebser, who speaks from the perspective of what I have been calling the emergent new consciousness. He says that we cannot foresee in detail what will come about, but things will by themselves come in the right way. We cannot speak of it in detail because we are dealing with a dimension beyond concepts. Unfortunately many people are not yet in the position to accept this.

I received a letter from a person who heard one of my talks in Germany said, "We Christians do not need all that emptying business—we already have Christ!" It was a very polite letter, but unfortunately I think it missed the point, for "Christ" here can become an idol, a concept that we need to empty ourselves of precisely in order to meet the real One, in this world of emptiness.

Yamada Roshi: As I have said before, I am of the impression that Christianity is not at all the way I used to think it was, with just a rigid system of beliefs and concepts. There seems to be something there in common with what we are concerned with in Zen. Now in the many tasks we face in the world today, not any one of us can do the task alone apart from the others. We must join hands in bringing about a world that is One.

RH: We are in a world situation that can be described well in terms of the Burning House Parable in the Lotus Sutra. This is a scenario wherein the children of the Buddha are depicted as little children playing with their toys in a house that is already burning. But being rapt in their play, they do not realize the danger they are in. The Buddha is likened to the children's father, who is outside the house, and is trying to call their attention to the situation, calling them to come outside and join him, but they do not hear him.

In this way, our living place called this Earth is about to crumble, with continual violence going on based on all kinds of ideological and even religious conflicts, with the increasing gap between the rich and the poor, and with ecological disasters that are in great part human caused. And yet we are still wallowing in our ignorance, concerned only with our petty selves and our little selfish games. With the realization of what Father Lassalle calls the new consciousness, or in other words, with the emptying of this petty self-centered "subjective consciousness" toward the manifestation of what Yamada Roshi calls the Essential World, the world of emptiness and thus precisely the world of Oneness, perhaps a way out of this Burning House will make itself apparent.

Recommended
Readings

THERE ARE MANY INTRODUCTORY BOOKS and manuals on Zen practice currently available, but for those who wish to read more about
the Zen style of the Harada-Yasutani-Yamada and Sanbo Kyodan
lineage, the book *Three Pillars of Zen,* edited by Philip Kapleau, might
be a good place to start. Robert Aitken's *Taking the Path of Zen* is an
excellent account based on the same tradition. Taizan Maezumi and
Bernie Glassman's *On Zen Practice: Body, Breath and Mind* is a valuable
collection with helpful accounts of elements for beginning practice,
also describing what is involved in *shikantaza* ("just sitting") and koan
practice. It also contains an important essay by Koun Yamada, entitled "Is Zen a Religion?" which is a refreshing treatment of the
interreligious possibilities of Zen practice and experience. John
Daishin Buksbazen's *Zen Meditation in Plain English,* and *The Art of Just
Sitting,* a collection of pieces by Zen masters from ancient China to
contemporary America, edited by John Daido Loori, are also very
helpful guides for beginners in Zen practice.

At our Maria Kannon Zen Center, the contents of our introductory talks are presented in *Beginning Zen,* available through www.mkzc.org. For treatments of koans, *The Gateless Gate* by Koun Yamada gives the reader a glimpse of this great twentieth-century Zen master's boundless mind and heart. Robert Aitken's *Gateless Barrier* is also a helpful guide to this classic collection first issued in China in the thirteenth century. Yamada's Zen talks on the koans of the *Blue Cliff Record* have been published in German translation, and an English translation is forthcoming from Wisdom Publications.

There are also a good number of books now published on socially engaged Buddhism. In particular, I recommend Ken Jones, *The New Social Face of Buddhism,* a revised version of the author's earlier book on socially engaged Buddhism, and David Loy's *The Great Awakening,* a very insightful presentation of social theory based on a Buddhist vision of reality. Specifically on Zen and social engagement, Christopher Ives's *Zen Awakening and Society* is notable. My own *Healing Breath: Zen Spirituality for a Wounded Earth* is likewise one attempt in articulating the socioecological dimension of Zen experience and practice. For books on Zen and Christian spirituality, Father Hugo Enomiya-Lassalle's works were pioneering, and most were published in German, but *The Practice of Zen Meditation* and *Living in the New Consciousness* are available in English. Robert Kennedy's *Zen Mind, Christian Mind* and *Zen Gifts to Christians* are musings on Zen and Christian spirituality by a Jesuit priest and Zen master. Sister Elaine MacInnes's *Light Sitting in Light* and *Zen Contemplation: A Bridge of Living Water* are very readable, personal accounts by a Catholic nun and Zen master who was also longtime director of Prison Phoenix Trust, a privately funded group that teaches meditation to interns in the British penal system. *Beside Still Waters,* edited by Harold Kasimow, Linda Kepplinger Keenan, and John Keenan, is a collection of essays by Jews and Christians whose lives have been influenced by Buddhist practice.

Japanese Jesuit priest and Rinzai Zen master J. K. Kadowaki's *Zen and the Bible,* translated by Joan Rieck, offers insightful reflections on koans and resonances with Biblical themes from the author's personal experience. Another Jesuit priest, William Johnston, has written numerous works on Mysticism and Christian spirituality that contain many descriptive references to Zen. In particular, his *Christian Zen* encourages Christians in this Buddhist meditative practice and offers helpful theological perspectives on Zen themes. Tom Chetwynd's *Zen and the Kingdom of Heaven* is a thoughtful work also deserving mention. For a well-known Buddhist's take on Christian themes, the Dalai Lama's *The Good Heart: A Buddhist Perspective on the Teachings of Jesus* is a refreshing read.

Index

About the
Author

RUBEN L.F. HABITO is the author of numerous publications, in both
Japanese and English, on Zen and Christianity and is a prominent figure
in the Buddhist-Christian Dialogue. A native of the Philippines, Habito
served as a Jesuit priest in Japan under the guidance of the great spiritual
pioneer Father Hugo Enomiya-Lassalle and studied Zen with renowned
teacher Koun Yamada. He lives in Dallas, Texas.

Wisdom Publications

WISDOM PUBLICATIONS, a nonprofit publisher, is dedicated to preserving and transmitting important works from all the major Buddhist traditions as well as related East-West themes.

To learn more about Wisdom, or browse our books on-line, visit our website at wisdompubs.org. You may request a copy of our mail-order catalog on-line or by writing to:

Wisdom Publications
199 Elm Street
Somerville, Massachusetts 02144 USA
Telephone: (617) 776-7416
Fax: (617) 776-7841
Email: info@wisdompubs.org
www.wisdompubs.org

The Wisdom Trust

AS A NONPROFIT PUBLISHER, Wisdom is dedicated to the publication of fine books for the benefit of all sentient beings and dependent upon the kindness and generosity of sponsors in order to do so. If you would like to make a donation to Wisdom, please do so through our Somerville office. If you would like to sponsor the publication of a book, please write or email us at the address above.

Thank you.

Wisdom is a nonprofit 501(c)(3) organization affiliated with the Foundation for the Preservation of the Mahayana Tradition (FPMT).

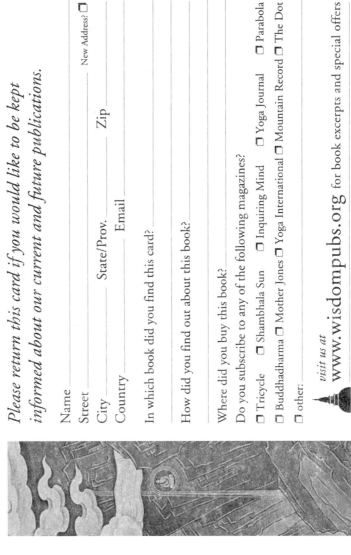

Please return this card if you would like to be kept informed about our current and future publications.

Name _____ New Address? ☐

Street _____

City _____ State/Prov. _____ Zip _____

Country _____ Email _____

In which book did you find this card? _____

_____

How did you find out about this book? _____

_____

Where did you buy this book? _____

Do you subscribe to any of the following magazines?

☐ Tricycle ☐ Shambhala Sun ☐ Inquiring Mind ☐ Yoga Journal ☐ Parabola
☐ Buddhadharma ☐ Mother Jones ☐ Yoga International ☐ Mountain Record ☐ The Dot
☐ other: _____

visit us at
www.wisdompubs.org for book excerpts and special offers

Wisdom Publications is a nonprofit charitable organization.

WISDOM
PUBLICATIONS

199 Elm Street · Somerville MA 02144 USA

Place
Stamp
Here